MUSLIMS LIKE US

MUSLIMS LIKE US

✦

A Bridge to Moderate Muslims

David J. Roomy

iUniverse, Inc.
New York Lincoln Shanghai

MUSLIMS LIKE US
A Bridge to Moderate Muslims

iUniverse books may be ordered through booksellers or by contacting:

iUniverse
2021 Pine Lake Road, Suite 100
Lincoln, NE 68512
www.iuniverse.com
1-800-Authors (1-800-288-4677)

ISBN-13: 978-0-595-35606-5 (pbk)
ISBN-13: 978-0-595-80087-2 (ebk)
ISBN-10: 0-595-35606-0 (pbk)
ISBN-10: 0-595-80087-4 (ebk)

Printed in the United States of America

Contents

INTRODUCTION

It is absolutely vital to the interests of North America, and Europe, to build a bridge to moderate Muslims. We share much in common—deep cultural values and, ultimately, our desires for peace. Hence our title: Muslims Like Us.

Have you ever awakened after an afternoon nap and discovered that the mind is actually free of pressure and preoccupations? For only as we know this supreme experience can we look upon all our problems, personal and collective, with equanimity. It is only then that we can take action, in a troubled world, with balance.

Others have such a mind, we all do. All human beings, potentially do. This is the point of meeting with others however different they may seem. In this book we see how brightness and freshness of mind characterized the rich tales of the Arab and Middle Eastern traditions. This can be a point of meeting between Westerners and Muslims.

As a psychotherapist working with people's troubled states of mind I have discovered that it is possible for such states to subside, and to be replaced with confidence, insight and creativity.

In some ways a group behaves like one individual, sometimes split, sometimes united. Expand that analogy to the world level, and you have our current situation; it is both split, and has within it the possibility of healing.

For a short time after the events of September 11, 2001, there was the possibility of a new world consciousness. A sharing of views and insights from many cultures and parties transpired. Citizens around the world had also been mobilized. All this brings about the possibility of being more of a world community, and more consciously so. And it means the necessity of hearing all the parts.

That possibility seems tested, even shattered. And yet, at such a dangerous time as this, there may still appear in people's minds and hearts, new ways to approach the "other" and to heal the split. Our discussion together in this work will be to unfold dimensions of that process.

Many times the proposed "action" may also be a shift in the attitude. Attitudes, like motivation, determine where the mind is being lead. Attitudes, when balanced, unfold in balanced action.

Here are some possible steps:

- be aware of what you are feeling even if it is disagreeable;
- be aware that you, too, have a shadow;
- know that the "others" may also represent parts of oneself one does not accept;
- be aware that bliss releases creativity toward personal groups and world problems;
- know that communication means exploring what is behind another's actions rather than assuming we know their meaning;
- speak to the leaders;
- regain more freedom of speech;
- avoid propaganda (look what it did to the people of Germany).

One step is exploring psyche's mercurial qualities. It is an ear to the ground listening for the possibilities still emerging for being on better terms with other members of the world community, and sitting with them at the world table.

With the chapter "One World", we consider a whole new framework for viewing our bodies, emotions and sexuality. But the implications of this new worldview, born of the new physics and in-depth psychology, are still more far-reaching. They include our relationships with all "others," in short, virtually everything. This chapter provides a philosophical basis for a whole new approach to improving cross-cultural understanding.

In "Helping to Avert Nuclear War" (Chapter 2), we open up alternative ways to the tendency to falsely split reality between "us" and "them." We avail ourselves to a facility of apprehending reality that is, at once, broader than reason yet includes reason. This facility is vital in a technological age when reason on its own can take us dangerously beyond our basic human reality and our natural connection with others.

In Chapter 3 we see how one person, William H. Kennedy, made a difference in the world when it was on the brink of nuclear war in the Sixties.

Next our discussion is "Muslims at the World Table." If the Muslims are not full members, then non-Muslims contribute to a situation that forces members of this religion/culture into being partial outsiders. It is easy to project negativities on outsiders, and those in that unfavorable position can be expected to also project negativities on the dominant culture. (Terrorism should be regarded as a special case and not as arising out of Islam.) Having a more enlightened view toward Muslims may or may not affect terrorists. But, at least, we in the West can affect the terrorists' milieu and potential support there. *We can align with moderate Muslims rather than alienating them.* They are important for our future and our security.

In the interest of creating further knowledge of Muslim culture, I introduce several writings (Chapters 4-6), that appreciate the wisdom of a portion of Islamic literature, namely the *Tales from the Thousand and One Nights.* There we may discover some of our common values. We may discover, indeed, that Muslims are like us. We meet there one of the great figures of world drama, Shahrazad, who has just that capacity of transforming men's warring tendencies into something sane, humane and of enriching life with imagination. I have tried to show how the wisdom of that secular literature, may be able to help us in these times with their depressive and anxious moods and with a creative response to the difficulties facing the world. The chapter "Experimentations with Shahrazad" develops the eros quality of Islamic culture (as different from the logos quality developed in the West, in C. G. Jung's view). The Sufi poet Rumi gave expression to that eros attitude to life.

It is extremely important to state that my treating the *Tales from the Thousand and One Nights* offers but one example of Muslim culture. This example and others mentioned by me are far from exhaustive. Indeed, being a "Muslim" means different things in different parts of the vast world inhabited by this great world religion of Islam. Sometimes in the West we may get the totally erroneous impression that Islam is a homogenous entity, whereas vast differences exist in this diverse community among the world's peoples. At times, too, we in the West may receive the false impression through the media that Muslims seem to be involved in a wholesale rejection of the West, whereas some of our Muslim friends may be counseling us that they are reacting to atheism and materialism.

Finally, we consider a motif from the West, the Holy Grail (Chapter 7). Here we approach a potential point of meeting between Christian people around the world. This group, too, is split, as conservative and liberal Christians are deeply suspicious of each other and sometimes hostile. Conservatives and liberals, whatever the issue, may find points of meeting if they go deeper. There is another reason for considering the Grail. It bespeaks a point of view that goes beyond reason and yet includes it. Such a framework may yet help to avert massive destructive tendencies in our world. We must give such alternatives a chance. They beckon towards a more holistic future for "one world". Also, a surprise may be in store for some regarding the origins of the Grail legend.

I shall end this introduction by telling how words and pictures burned in me as I sat by a fire and recalled the dream of the night before. It was that terrible, pregnant time just before the Gulf War. The second part of this poem, where I speak about a Greek priest, refers to seeing in the dream, the rift between life and death; I was seeing a scene similar to Rafael's painting of "The School of Athens," in which all the great philosophers, poets, and poetesses of antiquity, are gathered.

Revelations by the Fire

As the log opened fire bright,
there in the cave-like hearth
the brightest light
dios prepared to announce
its surprises in the world

The worst news
dios might still turn 'round.
An intuition like this, the hottest flame,
brings inside me, a child, and joy.

World's sufferings
beyond me.
I can't contain,
Only one big as the world
can.

Dios eternal in the flame
in the world
and in the heart
can
Kyrie Eleison.

Open hearth
open me

to what is newly
arising in me…

This the wise man
old and green
wearing moss on his sleeve
who met me in a dream,

Just before the crossing
where the road
widened
past the wood,

And I knew
he had been preparing
some courses for me
just by his Way,

What lay before me…
more, more Being like his,
more ripening,
his preparing,

I remembered the way
through a second wood
to the quiet garden
with the lily'd pond center

To the place of learning
the Wise Old Man's school
where quiet is contained in knowledge
of the Self within.

The mystery is there
he's waiting in the woods,

fire ready to burn
child to be born.

By the crossing
before the step I found
a wood growing
a long staff

Like the walking sticks
by Jung's door
opening into
the guide's house.

Woodsman, then like Jung,
the step beyond
opening
into the Greater Way

Were I to tell you
of the favors dios gives his children
you'd see the fire,
as these other dreams, too
dios gave to me:

The Greek priest
about third century
in the portal I passed
glanced barely at me.

But I saw
he had my face,
the thinker
with consummated glance.

Then my vision reached
that rift beyond

o'er which it is said
none passes nor returns,

Glimpse beyond of afterlife
spellbound faces
celebrating,
bright garmented,

Ancients and moderns,
poets, philosophers
schooled in Athens.
How could I return?

The dream did, to move to modern day;
before my group
was to start,
I stopped by the Greek Church.

No longer leaning by the door
I took a seat,
they all were filled,
in the holy assembly

The procession began,
was it Christ's
or Saint Nicholas
Rescuer from perils, joyful?

Beside him flaming
haired woman or man or
Archangel Michael,
and I woke on Christmas morn.

A deeper reality
dreams me,
I have seen his face
face as of the living priest

of the living dios, or All.
Does that living reality
yet burn a miracle
for all who yet stare into its incandescent glow—
World waiting
in us
to heal itself? [1]

Note:

1. David Roomy, *Inner Journey to Sacred Places*, Pentland Press, Raleigh, N.C., 1997, pp.44–48.

1

One World: its Philosophical Underpinnings

Unus mundus is one world lying beneath and common to manifestations as matter and spirit. C. G. Jung was talking about this theory right to the end of his life. It figured prominently in his discussions and correspondence with Wolfgang Pauli, the physicist and one of the originators of quantum mechanics.[1] This chapter is aimed at relevance for living. The theory of the *unus mundus* is key to that.

C. G. Jung, along with Sigmund Freud, was one of the great founders of Western psychotherapy as we have come to know it in modern times. Jung, 1875 to 1961, was a psychiatrist who proposed new methods of treatment paying particular attention to what he called the collective unconscious or objective psyche. The impact in recent times of his thought has been great in such diverse areas as psychotherapy, literary criticism, religion and mythology.

"Wholeness" is one of the ways Jung formulated the goal of his life. It means to be in relation to all aspects and dimensions of one's self. It is the aim of Jung's own individuation process. Wholeness is contrasted to the goal of being perfect and includes having a relationship with all the opposites in one's self, e.g., up and down, dark and light, etc. Not only is wholeness unfamiliar to many people in the area of ethics, but also in the theory of knowledge. In a left brain sort of way, we have been taught that if you take one position theoretically, the opposite must be false. William H. Kennedy, who was one of the first to apply Jung's ideas to world politics was fond of saying that we have not arrived in general consciousness to the position that there can be two rights.[2] Kennedy's insight is strategically important during this time of tension between the Western and Muslim worlds.

This value of wholeness is one of the marks of the God-image in us. In fact, Joseph Campbell, the great mythologist, feels such inclusiveness will be one of the qualities of the new religion as it emerges, much in the spirit of Kennedy's research. Facetiously, I say, "Where are we, if we cannot regard our ethical positions and our knowledge positions as ultimate?" Perhaps we are approaching that *unus mundus* of which Jung spoke. He said that consciousness necessitates our splitting of our world. But in psychology, Jung was a rare bird who posited something beyond consciousness, namely, the unconscious. He acknowledged that a person must split this world in order to perceive it, but that is not to say the way the world really is.

Let me give an example. Some people are oriented toward their sensory experience, and others toward meaning hidden in the depths. The difference in the whole person is that she or he perceives both. The whole person is aware that he or she is splitting the world in order to perceive it; but that the world itself, in itself, is one world, the *unus mundus.*[3] In this way, the opposites are united in the whole person. The unus viewpoint does not just mean the opposites are brought into relation to each other. It says that there is something more fundamental at work.

At the *unus mundus* level then the opposites are not the polar or dual realities we identify. They are rather "one". They are only manifested as spirit or matter, wave or particle, to our cognition.

How is the *unus mundus* manifested? I want to tell a story about Bill Kennedy. Bill "played a role on the world stage." This story took place in the 1960's and the height of The Cold War. Bill and I worked together on a daily basis for six years. It was after work one day when we had been meeting with an official of the Carl Duisberg Society, that Bill suggested that he and I have dinner in a simple Greek restaurant in Hell's Kitchen near 8th Avenue in New York. After dinner we sauntered along the streets. At a street corner, a man came up and addressed Bill. He was disheveled in dress and had a bottle in a paper bag. He offered Bill a nip from the exposed neck of the bottle. Bill declined. But then the man, who by this time had seemed to be very comfortable in Bill's presence, said very graciously, "please come back to my room with me, and we can talk". The man pointed to a typical building there in the very poor Hell's Kitchen neighborhood—his home. What I saw before my eyes was this: in the self-same way that I had seen Bill interact with top government officials, generals, famous writers and Jungians, I saw him react with this man. It was not patronizing. There was no high, low. Bill graciously and with deep respect indicated how much he would have liked to accept the man's offer to us but that we were already committed to something else that evening. The opposites were not split. Bill, with his aristocratic past, was at one with this man who was down and out.

If you take the *unus mundus* as the reference point, then you can talk about the three other qualities comprising our discussion, in a particular way:

1. body is not just body, but body/psyche

2. emotion is keyed into the psychoid layer of the psyche, a layer where psyche and matter are one;

3. sexuality, sensuality is not just an end in itself but a unification concept. Sexuality and sensuality are ways of being in touch with the *unus mundus* in the moment.

For a person who is already approaching completeness in any of these three areas, then any such area would not be what is needed for that person's wholeness. It might be something else which is needed. However, these three areas would be regarded as typically incomplete in a lot of people in our Western culture today. Each person would need to derive his or her own list of areas on this subject of what is not whole in himself or herself.

Now we shall attempt to go into each of these three areas. The body, the emotions, sexuality and sensuality. First, the body. If you watch the film, "Dr. Carl C. G. Jung <or> *Lapis Philosophorum*,"[4] you may get a sense of Jung's being grounded in the body. The body has come into psychotherapy in the last few decades, although you can trace it in Jung's work in the *Tavistrock* lectures and his comments on active imagination. For example, Emma Jung and Edith Wallace used dance for Edith Wallace's analysis.

In Process Work, which has its roots in Jung, I see how important it is to bring the body into therapy. First of all, clients would have to feel comfortable in going beyond talk therapy and involving the body directly. Such a therapeutic approach means, for those clients who are comfortable with it, following the psyche as it moves through physical movements, gestures and symptoms. In my experience, such following is part of the psyche being free to "move" and express itself.

Now with the body, it would be possible to have yet another split. We could regard the body as somehow the only reality. Further, that view could also be attached to a materialistic bias. That is, the body is only the body, meaning cells, atoms, genes, neurochemical processes. Such views, in their essence, might be based on views prior to the new physics. There, in the uncertainty principle, Werner Heisenberg posited that the human observer affects the behavior of electrons. This means, in effect, those psychic realities affect the so called material ones. So either way you have it (if you disregard the body or make it a thing in itself) there could be a split.

A split is in:

1. a view of the nature and treatment of diseases and disorders which is fundamentally one sided or materialistic, not taking into account the psychophysical unity;

2. an enthusiasm in body things as the answer.

By contrast, we have Jung's attitude toward his heart attack. Before I get to that...a word about attitude. Jung placed a great emphasis on attitude. It's not just what you do, but your attitude which is also important. Attitude really points to consciousness and being aware. In this topic we are exploring attitude, taking into account the *unus mundus*, which may be useful for living. C. G. Jung was taking care of himself and following medical advice after his heart attack and he was seeing his condition, his heart attack, in the one world attitude of *unus mundus*. He wrote to Wolfgang Pauli that he saw a synchronicity in his heart attack. That is, he says it is on the level of the *unus mundus*, which is the foundation of synchronicities.

In synchronicities, space, time and substance, and the human psyche are still at the unified level. This is also what Jung calls the psychoid layer of the psyche. The psychoid level is beneath our knowing. At that level the world is one. Psyche is not distinct from matter. At the psychoid layer, the archetypes per se, exist.

How is the psychoid layer of the psyche manifested in life? I want to speak of an experience of this before we return to Jung's mention of his heart attack as a synchronicity.

Once I had a client who did not have long to live. Nevertheless, a decision was made to amputate one of his limbs as it was cancerous. I wasn't happy with this, but it was outside my power to stop it. He had the operation, and for all I knew he was recovering nicely. He had returned from hospital to his room. I called in on him one day; in fact, I was seeing him more or less every day. But this particular day, I went home, and that night I had a dream.

I dreamt of him. In the dream, his limb was restored. And he was playing ball with a friend of his, whom I knew. In fact, the limb of my client and a limb of his friend were tied together, and on this they were getting around together.

They seemed to be having a great time playing soccer. And they were kicking up the dust, and as the dust particles began to fall back to earth, I saw the particles were gold.

On the next morning when I returned to work, I learned that this client had died during the night at about 5:00 a.m., the same time I had had the dream.

I believe in the dream, when I saw his limb restored, that I was seeing his "resurrection body", as Marie-Louise von Franz calls it.

So here is a master in psychological knowledge who has a heart attack. Yes, the heart is a pump, and it is a psychophysiological reality. In addition, it was for Jung in his heart attack, a manifestation of the one world of *unus mundus*. That was his attitude. The master is applying his theories to himself. You see if you or I had a heart attack, it could be regarded as simply concerning our precious person as seen in terms of the medical model. But for Jung, the event is meaningful at a transpersonal level. This is the level where the psyche and body are indistinguishable. For Jung, as he returned from the near-death experience he was able to go even deeper into psyche, and this gave him grist for the writing which followed, culminating in some of his greatest work.

I believe the proof of the pudding is when you can apply your theories to yourself. Jung did that in the instance cited.

This redefines wholeness, too. Wholeness is not just the unification of opposites like psyche and body, or spirit and body. But wholeness, for me, means an attitude to a pervasive, all encompassing whole, which is beyond the opposites, namely the *unus mundus*. Jung's term of the self is a manifestation of that larger reality. There is a therapeutic implication to this. It could be called the larger perspective. The latter is one meaning of healing. Healing is related to its root word meaning, wholeness.

The story of the Grimm's brothers lives fascinated me. When Wilhelm Grimm was almost dying, the characters from the stories he had made notes on, came to him. They told him they needed him to live in order for themselves to be. This gave his life meaning, and pulled him through. He was later to write these fairy tales in full. This is not only the larger perspective, but the larger reality.

There is a parallel here to what Jung said about God needing human beings. We, as humans, express "God" and give form to reality. The archetypes of the collective unconscious are present in the characters and dynamics of fairy tales.

Process Work's term "dreambody" formulated by Arnold Mindell is in his language, "the body's role in revealing the Self."[5] This is further being accepted in

Jungian circles. Lopez-Pedraza is one such Jungian analyst whose book brings in this interest in emotion and body.[6]

Eliade writes: "Buddha revealed…that the cosmos is contained in <a person's> own body, explained the importance of sexuality, and taught him to control the temporal rhythms by disciplining respiration—thus he could escape from the domination of time."[7]

This unity of cosmos and body gives rise to the concept of the "subtle body". Jung refers to the unseen bodies in his image of the golden castle as he represented in his *Red Book*. In the subtle body, the opposites are joined, they are together.

Jamling Norgay was following in the footsteps of his famous father when he climbed Mt. Everest. He writes: "…the *lungta* represents the degree of positive spiritual energy and awareness that propels people—their level of divine inner support. Sherpas say that if their *lungta* is high, they can survive almost any difficult situation and if it is low, they can die even while resting on a grassy slope like Tiger Hill".[8]

The attitudes we have discussed are: *unus mundus*, wholeness, and body/psyche. Next we come to emotion. First, I shall stress the importance of emotion for psychotherapy and living. Then I shall try to see through the attempt to make emotion an ultimate quality. The same approach was used with body.

Jung writes: "It seems as if the Western mind had a most penetrating intuition of man's fateful dependence upon some dark power which must cooperate if all is to be well. Indeed, whenever and wherever the unconscious fails to cooperate, man <the human being> is instantly at a loss, even in his most ordinary activities. Failure of memory…interest and concentration—such failure may well be the cause of serious annoyance, or of a fatal accident, a professional disaster, or a moral collapse."[9]

Peter Schellenbaum writes: "This book is intended to bring the pain of being unloved back into the body, seeing through that pain right down to its existential depths, and admitting all its repercussions into awareness, so as finally to come free of it…..and the feeling of being unloved can be dissolved by living through the complete range of emotions involved, which the persons concerned have previously avoided."[10] "…Pressure creates anxiety, and anxiety confines life…"[11]

Peter Schellenbaum shows that if we follow pain, it leads to an image. For me this is one of the most salient features available in psychotherapy. If you can feel it, then an image will form. It's an attitude you can bring to your pain and other emotions. There are many ways to avoid pain. It can even be avoided in psychotherapy. Many will try to comfort others in pain. But it is perhaps more of a gift to them, to hear their pain, and not to try to give an answer. For there is no answer, at least in concepts. As the listener, we may be taken into our own pain. Then to be in that place with the others, re-focused in awareness of their pain, they may be seen. Being seen, they may be able more so to be with their pain. Pain, like the other emotions, moves on; it moves as the archetypal psychologists are fond of saying. But pain, when allowed to be experienced, will not destroy us. For then we get comfort from the archetypes, or the *Emmaus* Christ or Buddha. When we are in the complex our defenses, negative fabrications are blocked from our vision of God, Buddha-nature.

This is another incident I want to tell you about. A few years ago, I was in England visiting my Jungian friends there. My wife and I decided to spend about six days in a Tibetan Buddhist Center in Scotland. We had been there going on six days, when it became clear that Aknog Tulku Rinpoche, the abbot of the monastery, would see me on the seventh day. But we were scheduled to leave early the next day. When I explained this to the appointments secretary, she arranged for me to see him early in the afternoon of our sixth day. He had just returned from a trip the night before.

I had never met him before. I had not discussed with anyone what I was going to talk with him about; in fact I think I had in mind some questions to do with practice and the connection of psychology and Buddhism.

I went up to his domicile at the appointment time. He met me at the door, told me where I could leave my wraps, and then went on into the main room, while I shed shoes and jackets in the ante-chamber. When I walked in and sat down, he said something to me about the more general questions which I was considering. Without a word from me on the subject he touched right on a basic complex of mine. He said that if I feared getting the flu I was more likely to get it. I was so surprised that he could have reached this totally intuitively that his remark had quite an impact on me which was healing.

To me, as I reflected later, I thought of it as a synchronicity. That he should speak of what was really on my mind. It was like the old shrines of the God of healing, Asklepios in Greece.

There the pilgrim could be healed; it happened when the pilgrim had a healing dream or the priest or the priest's slave had such a dream. There was in that synchronicity the meaningful connection between the dream and the synchronicity. It was then that the larger one world was touched into.

This is exactly how I felt. For a short time after this meeting, I was in touch with that reality which includes the teacher, the student and my maladies. Having a glimpse of this other reality meant that these things felt like a whole different concept and experience of the way things are. What had mattered to me so much before, was now experienced differently because I was experiencing from another level. That was partly healing.

I wanted to touch on dreams and synchronicity as they express the *unus mundus*, and my example, although not a night dream, is meant to contribute to this.

Now to making something of an ultimate quality about one's emotions. That could be a mistake, too. In *The Four Themed Precious Garland*, the readers of this Dzog Chen text are taught that: desire can lead to enlightenment, and the two are not really separate. But only if you get the point that desire belongs to a world that will pass away. And only the one who knows the desire and knows its impermanence, knows his or her Buddha-nature. That Buddha-nature is the unpassing quality of consciousness, the mirror-nature of reality, its capacity to be known and for one to be at-one with the known. Desire, not permanent in itself, leads to enlightenment. "The delusions purified of such grasping are the pristine awareness. When you see the voidness of these simultaneously arising and dissolving obstacles that have been preventing your liberation and Omniscience and in this way, you realize your Buddha-nature".[12]

Lastly, we come to sexuality and sensuality. A.T. Mann and Jane Lyle, in their book *Sacred Sexuality*, write: "When we sense the unity of love, we are filled with the desire to overcome the lonely restrictions of duality."[13] "Eros…the power that forms the world by the inner union of separated elements."[14] "It's (sexuality's) sacred function is to bring the lower self into realization…On the highest level, both love and sex generate a profound godlike energy within a person…"[15]

It is wonderful to be in unity with someone. This can happen sexually. But it can also happen through eros, this is relatedness.

The implication for sexuality to be drawn from Pauli's grasp of the *unus mundus* might be this: a male person's fascination with the anima (feminine image in a male person) is a link to reality, to matter and to the soul. She unites these dimensions which is why this seeks to come to consciousness.

One of the hidden appeals of sexuality is precisely this one world; for, male and female are brought together. In same gender sexuality, opposites may be involved as well. There is *mana* or power in sexuality. This pertains to sexuality as regards a real or imagined partner, as well as in relation to oneself. Does that *mana* pertain to the object or to something behind the object? Well, both are possible. In the case of a real or imagined object, instinct is involved. Sexuality is one of the basic instincts according to Jung. And instinct and archetype are two poles of a single continuum. Von Franz writes that once an instinct has been satisfied, that will be enough. This means that if one enters an instinct like sexuality with full awareness, then it will have its own natural satiation point.

I want to come back to the focus of what is behind the object. Here we can really speak of *mana*. It is through the imagined object that we can get closer to this subject. *Mana* lies in the imagination. *Mana* pertains to archetypal experience. Here is "awesome wonder" as an old hymn phrases it. We have been talking about the psychoid layer of the psyche where these archetypes lie, so to speak. So it would be possible to experience the *mana* of sexuality without an outer object. Just as in relation to the imagined object. (I am using object in object relations language rather than implying a sexual object.)

But I want to use that point to suggest something further, to really go behind sexuality even further. Here I believe we meet the mysterious union which itself conveys the *unus mundus*.

Does sexuality, meaning all we have been talking about, need to be satisfied at least on an imaginal basis, for wholeness. Possibly yes. And you could say the same for many other aspects of the personality. And there is a vitality from coming to terms with one's wholeness. This is *tantra* in its pure sense. Lama Yeshe said that one of the reasons yogis or yoginis who lived in solitary isolation did not often experience loneliness is because the individual's practice was the union of male and female energies.

Sexuality, in the sense that I am presenting it, does not mean acting out. Acting out is a social work term for the irresponsible taking of one's feelings into actions which impact others. I don't believe in going about finding fulfillment along these lines, in a way that brings harm to others. The question of whether sexuality is enacted with another person or imaginably within oneself is a question to be raised in the individual heart.

A woman dreamed the following dream. She was married. She dreamed two suitors wanted to make love to her. She wanted to keep her commitment to her husband. She looked from a platform down on the two men. They were vying for her attention. One was an East Indian and very passionate; this was to be his first affair outside his marriage. He was shy about exposure. The other man was European. The woman was trying to make a plan to be with each of them at separate times.

She commented on the dream: "it was a breakthrough because I wouldn't have done this in real life. And I was amazed at the quality of myself opening up." The woman who had this dream was able to find the meaning of it on an inner level. Jung developed this capacity in his clients through the use of active imagination. He writes: "The autonomous activity of the psyche, which can be explained neither as a reflex organ of external ideas, is, like every vital process, a continually creative act."[16] If you recognize your own involvement, you, yourself, must enter into the process with your personal reactions, just as if you were one of the fantasy figures, or rather, AS IF THE DRAMA ENACTED BEFORE YOUR EYES WERE REAL. It is a psychic fact that this fantasy is happening, and it AS REAL AS YOU—AS A PSYCHIC ENTITY—are real.

You have to give yourself to the process to reap the benefits. It can, provided your ego is strong, mean entertaining some thoughts or feelings which you are sure you would not act out, in order to know their message to you. For this it is advisable to have had a lot of analysis or depth psychotherapy, or to have such a practitioner at hand.

The mind can play tricks on you. And, as one psychiatrist, analyst has said, there is a thin line between mysticism and mental disorders. Having said all that, I want to quote from C. G. Jung. He said that "the deeper he went into his own darkness, the greater the sense he had of Grace meeting him at each new level. Finally, going through all the levels, leads to something."[17]

If you are attracted to spiritual things, give yourself the license to go there and explore. In a man's eye, the woman is an image of the human being, a pointer to our being human. There may be a paradox in these two concepts. The *unus mundus* is part of my theology. It integrates body/psyche, emotion, sexuality. It is one.

Julian of Norwich (1343-1415) says: "In the self-same point where the soul is made sensual, in the self-same point is the city of God ordained from without beginning."[18]

In another rendition of her words, we find: "For I saw very surely that our substance is in God, and I also saw that God is in our sensuality, for in the same instant and place in which our soul is made sensual, in that same instant and place exists the city of God."[19] This topic of the celestial city has interested me greatly for many years. My second book *Inner Journey to Sacred Places*[20], is an exposition of that image. Jung says the image of the ancient city is an offshoot of the *heiros gamos*, or sacred marriage. That *heiros gamos* is fundamental to our third sub-topic, sexuality or sensuality. In this way, we see that the *heiros gamos* is fundamental to sexual experience, real or imagined. An image of the mysterious union is, for one thing, an image of the union of the conscious and the unconscious.

As with body and emotion, we attempt to see through sexuality as taken to be an ultimate category. The key to this is the one world, the *unus mundus*. Sexuality and sensuality are holy, but they are not everything. The self is everything.

It's your attitude which is important, not just what you do. If you decide to do something, it is still the attitude which is important, as well as the event. A person can have a dream to take a trip. He or she can take the trip, or perhaps they don't need to go. The trip or journey is an inner reality. If one can get behind the impulse to make a particular journey and learn what it is which is pushing them in that direction, then one can arrive at consciousness. That consciousness can be taken up into a conscious attitude toward what one is doing, in this instance, a journey.

Attitude affects all the ways we live. Attitude comes into being by taking into account the reality of the psyche in which we live. In that attitude the psyche is seen as reflecting the *unus mundus*, and thereby a potential guide.

Attitude is so vital to cross-cultural encounter. The *unus mundus* means that we are all in this world connected within some deeper reality, call it the soul of the world. We, and all of those who are different from us, are connected there. All those other people, too, have manifestations of the highest striving of human culture e.g., the image of God in the human soul, and we all have our darkness, too. In our next chapter we shall explore how we can connect with that underlying reality through night dreams in ways that may enlarge the prospects for communication and peace.

Notes:

1. *Atom and the Archetype: The Jung/Pauli Letters*, 1932-1958, ed. by C. A. Meier, preface by Beverly Zabriskie, Princeton, Princeton University Press, 2001.

2. William H. Kennedy in a private remark, during 1960's.

3. Meier, ed., Ibid., p. 157.

4. Jonas Mekas, "*Dr. Carl C. G. Jung* <or> *Lapis Philosophorum*," filmed in 1950 by Jerome Hill and ed. in 1991 by Jonas Mekas, Arthouse Videotapes, no. 11.

5. Arnold Mindell, *Dreambody: The Body's Role In Revealing The Self*, Santa Monica, Sigo Press, 1982.

6. Rafael Lopez-Pedreaza, *Dionysus In Exile; On The Repression Of The Body And Emotion*, Wilmette, IL., Chiron Publications, 2000, p. 36.

7. Mircea Eliade, *Yoga: Immortality And Freedom*, Princeton, Princeton University Press, 1958, p. 204.

8. Jamling Tenzing Norgay, *Touching My Father's Soul: A Sherpa's Journey To The Top Of Everest*, Harper San Francisco, 2001, p. 15.

9. C. G. Jung, *Psychology And Religion*, Coll. Wks., Vol. 11, New York, Pantheon Books, 1963, pp.491-492.

10. Peter Schellenbaum, *The Wound Of The Unloved: Releasing The Life Energy*, Shaftesbury, Dorset, Element Books, Ltd., 1990, p. 97.

11. Ibid., 101.

12. *The Four-Themed Precious Garland: An Introduction To Dzog Ch'en*, Dharamsala, Library of Tibetan Works and Archives, 1979.

13. A T Mann, *Sacred Sexuality*, Shaftesbury, Dorset, Element Books, Ltd., 1995, p. 9.

14. Ibid., p. 16.

15. Ibid., pp. 182-186.

16. C. G. Jung, *Psychological Types*, Coll. Wks., Vol. 6, para 78.

17. C. G. Jung, *Mysterium Coniunctionis*, Coll. Wks., Vol. 14, para. 753.

18. Mann & Lyle, Ibid., p. 6.

19. *Julian: Woman Of Our Day*, ed. by Robert Llewelyn, Mystic, Conn., Twenty-Third Publications, 1988, p. 5.

20. David Roomy, *Inner Journey To Sacred Places*, Raleigh, N. C., 1997.

2

Helping to Avert Nuclear War

The discovery of the unconscious has come at such a time as this, when humankind can destroy himself, Jung reflected.

It was Emma Jung, the wife of C. G. Jung, who wrote:

> In our time when such threatening forces of cleavage are at work, splitting peoples, individuals, and atoms, it is doubly necessary that those which unite and hold together should become effective; for life is founded on the harmonious interplay of masculine and feminine forces, within the individual human being as well as without. Bringing these opposites into union is one of the most important tasks of present day psychotherapy.[1]

There is more than an analogy between the private suffering of the individual and the dynamics of the international malaise. Human beings' suffering is the same process whether it be the splitting up of a couple or the breaking off of talks between the Super Powers. Psychologically speaking, something very similar has happened in both instances: a dissociation or even fission of forces which lie in a field of tension with each other. As we can learn more and more about the individual, let's say from the subject of transference, we learn that those to whom we are close, at least, participate in our field. With the advent of mass media we have to ask ourselves if something of the same is not also true of the totality of human beings, and for life on this earth for that matter.

The forces which lie in the individual sometimes go beyond the precise definitions of that person's body for example. This is expressive of the field theory of modern physics. Bodies are not precise masses of matter. Rather, as if seen on a grid, those dense objects we recognize as manifestations of bodies/psyche involve the intense intersection of energy and particles. It was the American psychologist William James who pointed out that "...the idea of the unconscious could itself be compared to the 'field' concept in physics."[2]

When I mention the unconscious I am really talking about dreams, certain fantasies, free art work, etc., as well as the experience of modern physics at the time in which important discoveries or breakthroughs are made. In her article, *Science and the Unconscious*, Marie-Louise von Franz discusses how many discoveries were made (after a lot of hard work had been done) by "an intuitive flash of insight." [3]

Jung writes:

> The 19th-century German chemist KeKule, researching into the molecular structure of benzene, dreamed of a snake with its tail in its mouth. (This is an age-old symbol; shown in the book footnoted below is a representation of it from a third-century B.C. Greek manuscript.) He interpreted the dream to mean that the structure was a closed carbon ring…[4]

Dreams, themselves, in my own empirical data, have made this point: they have made a person specifically aware of the death of a loved one, across the space of more than a thousand miles at the very time of death and without her having knowledge of the warning signs of grave illness in her loved one.

Dreams are a master expression of our connection to the "other". At that point, we become involved in a question of whether it is really other or whether it is ourselves. If we were talking simply of theory of dream interpretation, we could discuss this under the topic of interpretation on the subjective or objective level.[5] Those principles are still valid in our larger discussion of the unconscious as it applies to the dynamics of international malaise.

Let us pause for a moment and look at the question in terms of individual. Let's say that a woman's marriage partner appears in her dream. Now it is her dream; it is happening to her, and the partner is represented in a way that she sees and or experiences that other person. That is interpretation on the subjective level. Let us say now that she is also aware that he is sailing out of her life, blown by a ferocious wind, driven to the edge of the ocean in a small open skiff, where none can reach him. Then later she discovers in fact her mate has developed a terminal illness and is in fact being drawn to the deep by the death instinct. Therefore there is some correspondence between the subjective side as she experienced it, and objective component, not so well defined.

I am reminded of this dream of C.G. Jung's which is in the literature. It was 1913 during the Fall, and the thirty-eight year old Jung was feeling an immense pressure. It did not seem to be only his, but in the atmosphere of Europe. When he was on a journey he had a vision. West of the Alps most of that part of Europe was flooded. He saw floating thousands of bodies and the accoutrements of civilization.

It was a catastrophe, and two weeks later the vision was repeated. He couldn't imagine that the vision had to do with revolution, and concluded he may himself be experiencing a psychosis. He said the idea of war hadn't occured to him.

In 1914, during the early summer, there were three dreams that showed the whole of Lorraine covered in ice and deserted of people. He said that in the third dream, there appeared a tree. Although it had no fruit, its leaves had been turned into healing grapes. These he plucked and distributed to the waiting hands of a large crowd of people.

Jung wrote: "On August 1 the World War broke out. Now my task was clear: I had to try to understand what happened and to what extent my own experience coincided with that of mankind in general. Therefore my first obligation was to probe the depths of my own psyche. I made a beginning by writing down the fantasies which had come to me during my building game. This work took precedence over everything else."[6]

Perhaps you are thinking of other dreams which are more timely. Have you thought of some dreams which seem to have our present conflicts as a subject? Are there dreams, with which you are familiar, which seem to point conflagration on a global scale or fear of impending world conflict?

I think it would be very interesting to study our dreams at this time. How do they reflect on the possibility of nuclear war, on suspicions which lie at the root of international malaise, and the routes out of this conflict?

Jung continues this story in his autobiography. He said that only when World War I was over did he himself come out of the darkness. He discovered at that time that he was spontaneously drawing mandalas, circles divided into four quadrants, or variations thereof.[7]

Jung states further:

> As early as 1918, I noticed peculiar disturbances in the unconscious of my German patients which could not be ascribed to this personal psychology...There was a disturbance of the collective unconscious in every single one of my German patients...The archetypes I had observed expressed primitivity, violence, and cruelty...When such symbols occur in a large number of individuals they begin to draw these individuals together as if by magnetic force, and thus a mob is formed...but when the individual was able to cling to a shred of reason, or to preserve the bonds of human relationship a new compensation was brought about in the unconscious by the very chaos of the con-

> scious mind...New symbols then appeared, of a collective nature, but this time reflecting the forces of ORDER. There was measure, proportion and symmetrical arrangement in these symbols...They represent a kind of axial system and are known as MANDALAS...The integration of unconscious contents is an individual act of realization...Only relatively few individuals can be expected to be capable of such an achievement...The maintenance and further development of civilization depends on such individuals...their moral and intellectual horizon has been considerably enlarged by the realization of the immense and overwhelming power of evil, and of the fact that mankind is capable of becoming merely its instrument...[8]

Why the mandala? Jung discovered that the answer it gave created another center of the personality than the ego. That was all important. When the totality of the person could emerge, there was a new objectivity connected to the experiences of other persons at the same time as these world events, catastrophic in quality, and of personal events of isolation (the break with Freud and professional colleagues of the time), Jung's unconscious went about its own way producing mandala drawings. The drawings created and expressed a new center of the personality. As Jung said, the rest of his life, another forty-five years was to give expression to these experiences which had so tempered his twentieth century way of viewing the world. He called this central experience of the personality the "self", and the mandala had enabled him to discover it.

Of the self, Jung writes: I have chosen the term "self" to designate the totality of man, the sum total of his conscious and unconscious contents."[9]

Mandalas appear spontaneously at times of great upheaval in the individual. Jung does not deem a mandala dream of his patient as a regression, with the implied inferior adaptation and lack of efficiency. Rather, things start to improve for the person as a whole. Jung feels this may be a continuation in the modern person of a development going back to the Middle Ages or even early Christianity.[10]

These inner experiences are a tradition of search in Western Culture. They are present in the Gnostics, the alchemists, and in individuals in the present century life who take the trouble to find their inner life. If we yield to this process, we pick up the thread of cultural development of which we are a part.

It is true that the development of the intellect is part of Western Cultural life. But the intellect need not be alone. Our tradition also includes wisdom and imagination. We are not simply robots and machines. Our minds are the products of thousands of years of development. We yearn to carry on the evolutionary thread. Regrettably, many people appear to be uninterested in the history of our development or the prospect of carrying it on further in our own lifetime.

The dreams of modern individuals, when followed against the background of cultural developments, some of which have remained underground and suppressed, can lead to the further discovery and involvement in our own day, of the patterns of life and culture which have given us birth as human beings. That is why the dreams are not just products of personal life but can throw light on, as they are part of, our culture and therefore our future.

I really don't know the outcome of such an inquiry. I do believe it could be interesting. I am familiar enough with dreams to know that their messages sound a bell which goes far beyond intellectual cognition. Dreams touch the emotions, the feelings, the humanity in us. At times they do, in fact, through the unconscious, connect us to forces within collective humanity, not to mention our own bodies. Because of the peculiar connection with our times, other people and the patterns of human existence, dreams do resonate in the person to whom they are told. We need to be able to share our dreams with people in other cultures with whom we are in conflict. We need to be able to share our dreams with our leaders. Out of our authenticity something is communicated to the authenticity of "the other". *I have great reason to believe therefore that this collection of dreams and its summary of motifs and outcomes could resonate in figures involved in political life. We would be attempting to see if the unconscious is saying anything about the problem of war and averting it.*

This kind of research, of connecting inner images to political actions flowing from them, has been done in the past. I call to your attention the work of Harold Isaacs: *Scratches on our Minds: American Views of China and India.* Here is how Isaacs went about his study and what he found.[11]

Isaacs reports on interviews conducted for the Center for International Studies at Massachusetts Institute of Technology. The individuals do not represent a sample. Rather, they were selected as key individuals: 32 were nationally prominent; 77, professionally prominent and 72 were occupying significant portions for the purposes of his inquiry. The selection of individuals aimed at a balance of opinion on public issues and a balance of political identification. Among this group, a wide spectrum of images of the Chinese exist, from positive to negative. Isaacs shows how this assortment of varying images is drawn upon within changing circumstances. On the negative side, the faceless man characterized images given by fifty-five of the panelists. Isaacs quotes a description by the military historian S.L.A. Marshall 13 of an encounter by American forces with the Chinese army in Korea "...the American forces was swamped by a Yellow Tide which moved upon it from all sides." Isaacs notes further:

> The 'yellow tide' in Korea swept up all sorts of ancestral memories. The new images were built up swiftly, not only out of the reality of the new foe, but out of materials that had lain long in the recesses of time and the mind. The Mongol hordes had reappeared.[12]

The "human sea" imagery was active throughout the Korean War in the reporting, but at the end of the war, and later, it had been confronted by the reality of the Chinese Army as a technically-backed, modern force fighting with military sophistication.

Images shape events. Understanding images projected by the media, for example, can help us to enter events wide-eyed and perhaps to see what is really happening.

Looked at more bravely, we have a responsibility, with our knowledge from the human psyche, to bring this to bear on public life. We can compare our images from experience to what we can discover through the media about the people of other nations. This can only lead to further understanding.

Also, in the psyche is healing. The word healing is rooted in wholeness. The psyche incorporates all places and times; more specifically, the patterns of human existence that are found in all places and times. Wholeness means incorporating into our conscious understanding other ways of being that we cannot understand or easily accept from other cultures. Wholeness means to be alive to our own splits and foibles and also to the possible healing that is also often present...if recognized and lived. That means the imagination to do something about our future coupled with the most dynamic force available to us, the human psyche. As Jung said, "Man has nothing to fear but man himself".[13] The seeds of disarmament may lie in our psyches.

One of the roots of modern science itself comes from the psychological reflection and observation of the inner person as promulgated by John of Salisbury.[14] I propose this to be part of our study and reflection; to become aware of how our inner images shape our outer perceptions of outer "reality". For it is here that we can be manipulated by media. When media becomes overly linked to certain interests in a society, then large portions of whole nations can be influenced into having a singular, and sometimes blatantly inaccurate, view of specific world events and situations. U.S. President Dwight Eisenhower warned of the power of the military-industrial complex as such an interest group. Democratic freedoms long established in U.S. history, for example, can be seriously compromised in this way. For democracy to work, citizens must be exposed to pluralistic views, even opposing views, in order to ascertain and register their intelligent choice. If powerful special interest groups dominate the interpretation of the news from a single perspective, they end up robbing the citizenry of intelligent choice. How are we to learn more about the diverse cultures and views of Muslims around the world, for example? One thing within our power to do is to endeavor to meet and dialogue with Muslims in our own communities in North America and Europe. If we are part of a church or synagogue, we may be able to convince others of this worthwhile activity and enlarge the circle of informed engagement with others of different cultures. More positively, with creative imagination and input from dreams from the great psyche, we may bring about remarkable resolutions to world conflicts. As a practitioner of Jungian psychotherapy I have a vast experience of how much the psyche can speak to life situations. The psyche seems to be interested in wholeness and balance. It mitigates against one-sidedness with formidable power and truth. Then people gain consciousness of their own shadows and "evil", this has a liberating effect on all those around them. This impact can even be carried directly through the "field" of the collective consciousness which underlies our seemingly separate consciousness. I remember, for example, once when in one of my groups a woman spoke of a behavior of a friend which had been vexing her for years. When she got home that same evening, she found that the behavior had been changed by her friend already, without his conscious knowledge of anything that had happened in our group. After a soccer victory, I saw what seemed to be the whole population of Athens act as if of one mind. Subtle changes in the awareness of individuals can affect large groups and societies. Jung kept saying that the individual is the only carrier of consciousness.

Notes:

1. Emma Jung, *Animus and Anima*, New York, The Analytical Psychology Club of New York, Inc., p.87.

2. C.C. G. Jung et. al., *Man and his Symbols*, London, Aldus Books, 1964, p. 308.

3. Ibid., p.307.

4. Ibid., p. 38.

5. C. G. Jung, *The Structure and Dynamics of the Psyche*, trans. R. F. C. Hull, *The Collected Works* of C. G. Jung, Bollingen Series XX, vol. 8, Princeton, N.J., The Princeton University Press, 1969, p. 266 ff.

6. C. G. Jung, *Memories, Dreams, Reflections*, New York, Random House, Inc., 1965, pp. 175, 176.

7. Ibid., p. 195.

8. C. G. Jung, *Civilization in Transition*, trans. R. F. C. Hull, *The Collected Works of C. G. Jung*, Bollingen Foundation, 1964, pp. 219-221.

9. C. G. Jung, Psychology and Religion: West and East, trans. R. F. C. Hull, *The Collected Works of C. G. Jung, Bollingen Series XX, vol. II*, New York, Pantheon Books, 1963, p. 82.

10. Ibid., pp. 96, 97.

11. Harold R. Isaacs, *Scratches on Our Minds: American Views of China and India*, Armonk, N.Y., M.C. Sharpe, Inc., 1980, p.99.

12. Ibid., p.233.

13. *Face to Face*, B.B. C. Filmed interview of Jung conducted by John Freeman, 1959.

14. Wilhelm Windelband, *A History of Philosophy*, 2 vols., New York, Harper & Brothers, Publishers, 1958, p. 307.

3

What Can Really be Done in Improving Cross-Cultural Communication: The Story of William H. Kennedy

Cross-cultural encounter is one of the most important ways of working to diffuse tensions and hostilities in various places in the world. It means, in part, meeting people from cultures other than our own. However, something more is needed in this endeavor; we must practice the skills which will enable us to engage creatively with the cultural differences of the "other". I am proposing that North Americans find ways to so engage with Muslims within and without their borders. A man by the name of William H. Kennedy mastered this plan and put it in effect during the tense years of the Cold War. Perhaps his story will suggest possibilities in our time of tensions.

I first met William Kennedy, or "Bill", as he liked to be called, in September of 1963, during the height of the Cold War. The friend who introduced me to him told me Bill had grown up in C.G. Jung's home. I and many others felt that Bill, like Jung, was a great man. The particular project which Bill and I carried out has relevance to the creative impact of psychotherapy upon the problems of our times. I believe it to be an example of cross-cultural communication to hold before us.

Bill was a tall man, with reddish hair, an Ayrshire nose, and a strong handshake in combination with his obviously cultured demeanor.

How did Bill get to be doing a project in cross-cultural understanding at that time? Years later I found out that at least one of his life events which had figured into his then current work. He had attended, as an American youth, a private school in Switzerland and there had become life-long friends with people from Germany, France and England. Later, these close friends were to be in opposing camps during the Second World War, and large portions of their countries were decimated, as well as civil life as we know it. While Germany was still burning, Bill met a German friend, and in that meeting vowed that he would dedicate the rest of his life to preventing such destruction as had taken place in the war from ever happening again. He had some ideas of how that could be accomplished. In essence, he knew that if people from different cultures could learn to talk through their differences and conflicts, then war could be prevented.

Bill also knew the potential destructiveness of the human psyche. On another occasion for example, Bill recounted his experience of liberating a concentration camp. The horrors of World War II had burned themselves into Bill's consciousness. He had experienced in this setting of the Nazi cruelty and brutality to the Jews, an arrogant, cold attitude on the part of the prison guards. That he had been there and knew these things firsthand, gave his presence a quality of leadership which was undeniable.

Bill's life was lived at the epicenter of big events. These and other reasons made it reasonable that he would have a big impact. For example, just after the World War II, he was in charge of reorganizing the arts in Europe, especially the region of Bavaria. In this regard he met the great writers of several countries and enabled them to start publishing again. He could enlist almost anyone in his cause, though a personal charisma and greatness.

I will say that a passion for dedicating his life to the prevention of anything like the Second World War caught my deepest imagination when I met him in 1963. We became acquainted that first year, and in one year hence, I had began my work as his associate. The National Episcopal Church in the U.S. put the money behind the project. That was to last for the next six years.

Now what was that project? Bill had conceived this plan. The plan was to impact events in the world. And if such a strategy grows from a person's deep psychological understanding, as it did in the case of Bill, then it will have a good chance of being effective. In this instance, Bill conceived the project as a kind of extraverted Jungian analysis for those most deeply connected to it. Bill was totally devoted to Jung, and was concurrently devoted to the cross-cultural work. He was the President of the C.G. Jung Foundation of New York. (Following that first meeting with Bill I began analysis with Brewster Beach and then Esther Harding.)

How was this partly psychological plan to work? In 1963, the Cold War was still at its height. The Cuban Missile Crisis, you will recall, happened during the Autumn of 1961. Those facts were central because our program was going to invite intelligent, articulate graduate students from countries bordering on the

"Iron Curtain" in Europe, and from the Middle East. For the Americans those visiting students would be the "other". Those students would not have the same cultural assumptions as the Americans. Therefore, they would expose their American acquaintances to views and powers beyond American assumptions perhaps contributing to the Americans' psychological awareness.

Who were the Americans to be thus exposed? They were the presidents and leadership of U.S. corporations. Bill would repeatedly point out that this group was insulated from other points of view. Typically, they did not meet others outside their own circles, especially others who could enlighten them on the different perspectives such as of people just on the border between Western Europe and Eastern Europe including the Soviet Union. These countries also were known to be the area where informal, non-publicized talks could take place, where information, and perhaps mediation, could pass between the nuclear superpowers.

In one instance a student came from Austria to work in the company of a millionaire who owned a factory in one of the Midwestern U.S. states. One day the self-made man who owned this company called in the student. He asked his advice on the pricing of a new article. The student asked the costs of materials and production, let's say nine dollars. The student then proposed the mark-up to be six dollars, for a final price of fifteen dollars. The owner said, 'But I can get something like $45.00'. The student retorted, 'But that is immoral'. Bill and I had an international incident on our hands. The owner was outraged. Our project had come into being in order to utilize such conflict for increasing psychological and cross-cultural understanding in all the participants. We were also keen to develop communication skills for handling conflict by helping the participants work through such experiences. Could people learn to talk through cross-cultural differences and not have to go to war over those differences? The industrialist and the student learned, rather had the experience, that differences can be discussed and sometimes worked through. A mighty industrialist learned that assumptions that he had never questioned were just that. He realized he might have to examine his assumptions and those of the culture around him. This is related to what the psychiatrist, C.G. Jung would call examination of the shadow. Americans, at time, have been seen by people in other parts of the world to act in a high minded manner while at the same time concealing more self-interested motives. The industrialist had enlisted in a noble course of cross-cultural understanding by hiring the European student for the summer. What he had not reckoned with was that his commercial behavior could be questioned and found wanting, from another person's point of view. In the process of discussing their differences, the industrialist and the student arrived at a new, more balanced understanding of their issues and each other's points of view. Both men were changed and took their new perspectives into their respective worlds.

That was one of Bill's teaching tools. When the situation of difference arises, something like this form of dialogue can take place. One person, "A", says to person "B", "I noticed you did such and such an action. In my culture that would mean "X". However, what does that action mean in your culture?" Invariably, it is "Y", something different from what one's cultural assumptions would lead one to believe.

The two persons are confronted with each other's "otherness". Here, Bill had something salient to offer for a new awareness. He said, when we as two persons disagree, it can be possible that I am right and you are right. When such a point of view can permeate the awareness of persons in different cultures, it can offer the possibility of new ways to deal with difference and with conflict.

We can, I am sure, apply that to trouble spots in the world today.

There are some other things I would like to tell you about Bill. As I have already said, Bill, after World War II, had been asked by the U.S. Army to help reorganize some of the Arts in parts of Germany, and perhaps elsewhere. In this regard he met with famous writers of the time. (He was mentioned with gratitude for his work in a work *Tagenbuch,* a copy of which I secured for him in Paris in the late Sixties). He maintained contacts with these people later. When he would go to Paris in the sixties, he would be part of the scene with Jean-Paul Sartre and others.

His social life in New York included some of the aristocratic families. I remember in particular, he spoke once of Christmas dinner with an old friend from his private school days in Switzerland. A U.S. President of that time, the Sixties, was also there for dinner. It is my understanding that Bill himself was the grandson of William Henry Harrison, a U.S. President, hence Bill's full name, William Harrison Kennedy. These parts of his background highlight the unusual quality in this man in his open and respectful response to the down and out man in Hell's Kitchen in New York I witnessed.

Bill had a very deep knowledge of various European countries and cultures. Much of his younger life had been spent in Europe. He was fifty-three when I met him in 1963. He was fluent in the French and German languages. Bill had been a reporter for the *Toronto Star* after World War II, and had been detained and tortured in Moscow by the Russians. This privation may have been one of the reasons for his great love of the culinary arts and fine cuisine. However, it was always the company of his guests at extraordinary meals which captivated Bill's attention. His attentiveness to other persons was in my case unforgettable. Following the trauma of the war years and afterwards, it was Jung himself who had directed Bill to take up consultation with Esther Harding.

Bill and Esther Harding had a very special relationship. Dr. Harding had been a student of Jung's starting in the 1920's. She was one of the first three women doctors to bring Jungian psychology to North America. In the period starting around 1963, Dr. Harding was the chairman of the C.G. Jung Institute of New York while Bill was President of the Foundation. I recall their meeting weekly to discuss the big issues around these then emerging organizations.

During the Sixties, it was said that Bill contributed more to the spread of Jungian psychology in North America, than any other non-analyst. As I have said, he was devoted to Jung. He and Esther Harding inspired Centerpoint, founded by Chandler "Chink" Brown and Elsom Eldridge as part of the Educational Center in St. Louis. Bill regularly traveled out from New York to see and support individual analysts in cities throughout the U.S.

Bill's connection with Jung was particularly significant to me. My life long involvement in the Jungian field began after reading *Memories, Dreams, Reflections*, and then synchronistically meeting Bill. I am but one of many, many people who were started off on their path in this field by Bill. We owe much to Bill's encouragement and support in this venture which, for us, has been life enriching, to say the least.

Jungian psychology and the cross-cultural understanding which Bill and I wanted to foster, were intimately connected. He and I extended our cross-cultural programs throughout the U. S. In its last year of existence, we had about two-hundred European graduate students coming to the States, to work in companies and live with families. They were to learn more about how to communicate with someone from another culture where differences of view were involved.

I believe that our program was of service to the world which has emerged since World War II. The students in our program, whom we were able to follow years later, went on to assume roles of leadership in their home countries and, sometimes, internationally. To these positions of responsibility they brought an understanding of cross-cultural differences and the skills to deal with situations in which those differences arose.

A dramatic loss of income in our original sponsoring agency, the National Episcopal Church in the U.S., spelled the end of the formal program. Bill, and I, carried on our work independently. I became a faculty member of a world college sponsored by the Society of Friends and lived and worked in England for seven years.

4

Muslims at the World Table

Many years ago I saw a sociological chart about North Americans' prejudice toward various peoples of the world. In this chart Turkish, Arab, and Muslim people were among those for whom there was the greatest prejudice. I have felt that those who are shut out, so to speak, must feel this very painfully. It is also likely that such inner attitudes on the part of North Americans may have a way of producing further divisions and antagonism. It seems urgent that Muslims be invited to the world table with full benefits and respect. One way to start eroding the negative qualities of prejudice is to learn more about what those from Western cultures and those from Muslim cultures have in common.

From one of the sources of Islamic wisdom, the *Tales from the Thousand and One Nights*, we may draw some unusual insights. Like many fairy tales, this collection of stories points to conditions in which the archetypal powers of the psyche may be balanced. They may also show how much Westerners and Muslims share common values.

There is another important reason for utilizing the wisdom of the *Tales.* It is their intrinsic worth, as stories, representing the dynamics of the psyche. As Jung pointed out, the less conscious part of the psyche plays a role in relation to more conscious views; this role Jung characterized as being one of complementarity. *The Tales,* according to Dawood, represent the more secular side of Islamic culture. As good fairy tales they complement more rational, collective views held in many cultures. All these points about the *Tales* are related. The part that has been excluded is the part which is needed for wholeness: Islam is needed by the world, the secular is needed by the sacred, the imaginative story of the inner world is needed by collective outer points of view.

In writing this material on Arab sources, I had the encouragement that C. G. Jung admired Islamic culture in the value it gives to eros, or relatedness. I had a first-hand experience of this quality of people from the Middle East when I taught and counseled at a college in England. I found these young people to have a very sweet nature and liked them very much. Finally, I had an important dream in the late seventies in which Jung encouraged me to follow this interest in writing about the *Tales*. I turn now to the story of the great woman Shahrazad. Her story is the background for all the tales and for their telling.

The powerful king Shahriyar was enraged. In fact, both he and his brother Shahzaman shared this pervasive feeling.

Something had happened to each of them to shock their inner feeling. Shahzaman first witnessed *his* wife's infidelity; this led him to his brother's house, where he had discovered what he regarded as an even greater malaise than his own there. Curiously, this realization led immediately to the lifting of Shahzaman's depression.

Shahzaman who had first hoped to keep secret his own problem, eventually told his brother both of the discovery of his wife in the arms of a slave, and of King Shahriyar's wife in the sexual company of her ten females and ten slaves. Subsequently, King Shahriyar took on the depression.

Both men decided to leave their roles as kings, temporarily, and to steal into the world to get an impression of how others were faring, in order to have some comparison. It was in these circumstances that they met the great Jinnee in the form of a very large black cloud. This powerful figure kept his wife in a chest, but even so, she managed to seduce them among another ninety-eight men whom she had made love to right under her sleeping husband's nose. Both men were comforted, as they said: "If such a thing could happen to mighty Jinnee, then our own misfortune is light, indeed."

King Shahriyar, like his brother before him, returned to his castle and, armed with some insane impulse, slew his wife, as his brother had done before him. Thereafter, according to the story, the King took a new wife each night and slew her the next day, thus attempting to defend himself from further personal shame by any wife who might be unfaithful. But, his treacherous measures

only made his people groan under his despotic and psychotic behavior.

With such a great offense to the feminine and to human life, where could help come from? Only from another woman, as it was in the King's lack of a real connection to the feminine that his depression, and his murderous malady, arose.

What would this woman do for him?

The woman, Shahrazad, devised a plan for the restoration of the King and for the kingdom. She would become the King's wife. In the gathering of people about the King during the evening, Shahrazad would tell the King a story. Then, immediately after this story was concluded, Dunyazad, Shahrazad's sister, would say: "How sweet is thy story, O sister mine, and how enjoyable and delectable!"

Then Shahrazad would say: "And where is this compared with that I would relate to you on the coming night if the King suffer me to survive?"[1]

Such beauty and wisdom were in the stories and the telling, that this plan of Shahrazad worked not only on the first critical night, but each successive night, for a thousand and one nights. The greatest mystery of the tales is that they are really dreams. The King wishes to sleep and can't. In this vulnerability of insomnia in which he must admit his troubled unconscious and conscience, relief comes. Ostensibly, it is in the form of stories. As stories, the reader can first accept them and participate fancifully in them. But the stories are, in another respect, the King's own dreams. These he is given in place of his sleeplessness and anxiety. Shahrazad gives him dreams and sleep which heal him and bring him back to a restored condition. On the life side, she gives him three sons and companionship.

The story always moves me when I hear it or tell it. It is about an inner transformation, one of the most profound which can come to a man. It is about feeling, and as a tale it works on feeling, eros, and relatedness. Von Franz writes: "The anima is personification of...vague feelings and moods, prophetic hunches, receptiveness to the irrational, capacity for personal love, feeling for nature, and—last but not least—his relation to the unconscious."[2]

Shahrazad's tales, like the threads of continuous creative elements emerging from the unconscious in dreams and fantasies, offer the possibility of change and renewal. This is the value of inner work in the individual. As Jung, von Franz, and many of us have experienced, it is in the recording of dreams over a period of time and working on them, that the true healing effect of psyche can be felt. This leads to a new center of the personality, known as the self.[3] That self then speaks in the realization of the life dream or personal myth of the individual. The creative impact of the psyche can also be observed in personal relationships as conflicts, anger and resentments are worked through. These inevitably involve the discovery of more of one's own personal myth and the vital energy for living that myth.

The eros quality of Islam may serve to balance the more logos quality of Christianity and perhaps of Judaism as well.

This poem of mine was inspired by the writings of Nikos Kazantzakis, of Crete, where Arab and Christian influences mixed.

Cretan Beauty

The delicate body of the anima
walks within the lattice of the garden.
The Turkish chieftain has brought her
to his powerful Cretan palace.
She is not a lady of this place.
Circassian, she roamed on horse
in expanses outside her village
where a man was with a woman
when he wanted, and a woman
with a man, the same.
I drink to you, Turkish
princess afield in Crete.
Your chieftain knowing our weakness
has barricaded you from sight
and rightly so, yet some
can look upon pure beauty
and turn the sight to poem
and to them and to you
I wiggle open the lattice
to bring the sublime to view.

A person's soul or anima may be the *inspiratrice.* It means contacting the attraction one might have to the beauty of another person and recognizing that as one's own soul. That is the beginning of creativity and a necessary step to its realization.

The creative always involves contact with what is not so known. The anima is one inner figure which may help to mediate contact with the unformed chaos of the inner world or an outer situation. It was Rosemary Gordon who first suggested to me the idea of turning the attraction the eyes might have for an outer woman, into a poem.[4]

I add to these points about inner work and the anima this possibility: two people processing things in their relationship can be useful to their respective cultures and the world.[5]

I, too, see the world as many other philosophers have since ancient times, as a living whole. My own immortality partakes of that, for I belong to the whole. My dust particles and chemical elements partake of the building blocks up the universe. My culture belongs to the Chinese, the Arabs, the Greeks, the English, all. The part I have played in people's lives, lives on after me. Culture never dies, but rather evolves from the portions that each of us allow to accrue to its golden, festooned borders, like barnacles on old wharfs.

Ours is an ancient race, *Homo sapiens*—race not used in the strict sense of the anthropologists. Our race as a world of women and men resides permanently in the images which arise spontaneously in every culture, time of history and place. These are the archetypes of the unconscious, as Jung has described them. One such concept arising from an archetype is, as Joseph Campbell has pointed out, the belief that in some form life goes on after death.

Antoine, a friend, has a myth to bring healing, that is a perspective of wholeness, to world parts, estranged from each other. He is especially interested in the peoples associated with those cultures arising from the fertile Middle East, and the modern people who are linked to those ideas, either closely or from afar by participating in the modern cultures influenced thereby. Many people of good will will have motivations similar to Antoine. There remains the discovery of the means to bring estranged parts in touch with each other. Perhaps process oriented psychology is one such means.

As the ancient poet Rumi said, it is not possible to know the truth in a dispute till both parties are present. The dynamic system of process work can work with those opposing forces once they are in proximity to each other. Those methods of conflict resolution are part of our repertoire as healers.[6] Perhaps those in power, which to some extent is all of us, will see ways to become reconciled to all our parts, so that the world may truly become the whole culture that it is.

I have seen this reconciliation take place over and over again at various levels: within the individual, with people in relationship, between fathers and sons, in small work teams, in small groups and large groups. In our collective experience as process workers, our form of conflict resolution has been tried in some of the trouble spots of the world. Arnold Mindell and Amy Mindell have taken their "world work" to such troubled spots as Israel, South Africa, and the former Soviet Union. They have sustained very good results.

Among you, as readers, some will want to help heal the world parts. Perhaps that is so deep in your souls it may feel like part of your personal myth. But, how to help? Meditate on your personal myth. As Arnold Mindell says, if you take up your personal myth you will naturally occupy your part in the world field or whole. One's personal myth involves a search into the question of why did I come into the world. In trying to find one's personal myth, one asks oneself, what is the image which shapes my deep understanding of my role in the world.

Notes:

1. *Oriental Splendor*, ed. Herbert van Thal, London, New English Library, Ltd., 1962, p.40.

2. C. G. Jung, et al., *Man and his Symbols*, London, Aldus, 1964.

3. Ibid., p. 196.

4. Rosemary Gordon, *Dying and Creating, a Search for Meaning*, London, The Society of Analytical Psychology, 1978.

5. Arnold Mindell, *The Dreambody in Relationships*, London and New York, Arkana, 1988.

6. Arnold Mindell, *The Healer as Martial Artist: An Introduction to Deep Democracy*, Harper Collins, San Francisco, 1992.

5

Medieval Muslim Cultural Values in the Tales from the Thousand and One Nights

People fall on hard times. Oddly, there is something in human nature which shuns people in such a predicament. Our tale from the *Tales from the Thousand and One Nights,* "The Dream"[1] speaks to this condition. In brief, a merchant has lost his fortune. This is a story for the down and out. One suffering from a chronic low-grade depression or a feeling of loss of life in oneself.

A merchant has squandered his wealth and now could earn his living only by the hardest labor. He has a heavy heart. He has journeyed from Baghdad to Cairo.

The merchant can not afford to stay in an inn. He sleeps in the courtyard of the mosque. We would expect something beneficial to come of that. Instead, he receives a beating. But, as we are later to discover, it is in this way that he was in a position for other events to unfold, i.e. to meet a man who could give him a complementary dream. For the merchant, it was a near death experience as well.

Another element of these dream-like events is that the poor man is beaten up in the sacred precinct. This is very strange. We would expect him to have protection there in the courtyard of the mosque. This courtyard is what, in the language of depth psychology, is called a *tenemos.* It is a safe inner place. It's protection from outside influences give to this inner spot a concentrative quality in which a transformation can take place.

Here our former merchant from Baghdad becomes a victim. He is victim to the action of thieves, or more precisely, he receives what the thieves would have got if they had been caught. He is mistaken for one of the thieves. He is beaten up so badly by the police, that he nearly dies.

This is like a bad dream which follows a bad thing that has happened in outer life. The two events, one outer and one inner are very much the same. You remember the merchant has come to these hard times because he has squandered his wealth. It is as if a thief in himself, perhaps his own self-indulgence has "robbed" him of his wealth.

But now we have just spoken of the events in the courtyard of the mosque as if they are a dream. They were real. It is just that due to the quality of the *tenemos* present in this segment of the story and the similarity of the courtyard episode to the man's psychological condition, a dream like quality is suggested. However, as the story goes, it is action following on action. And, it seems, things must get worse before they can get better. Therefore, the beating following the merchant's being mistaken for the crooks is to the good in one sense: it leads in the sequence of events to the very truth which the merchant must learn if he is to be restored. It seems at times as if the illness or downward spiral must run its course and reach a sort of bottom (in the merchant's case, near death) before another trend can take place; this other trend will be toward life and renewal.

Pouring his story out to the chief of police, the merchant hears the chief's dream which complements his own dream-like experiences. How often is this the case? Very often, in my own experience, I have been puzzled about a dream image in the morning upon waking, only to find that later in the day, this image was made clear to me by a chance remark of someone. By the same token, it is not uncommon for a husband to dream his wife's dream. Apparently, the merchant and the police chief don't know each other, but they are close. They are bound to come into contact as two opposite elements: the merchant who has lost control and the police chief, who exhibits great control in the nature of his work. The police chief makes a chance remark about treasure being buried under a fountain in a garden, and he gives some particulars in his account to the merchant. This image of the fountain comes from a repetitive dream of his.

The merchant is open to the fact that this dream is talking to him, while the police chief, for all his control, is too solidly planted on the ground. He misses the meaning of symbols. He discounts dreams. This element of the police chief has only a limited usefulness to the merchant from Baghdad who is quietly waking up to his new possibilities. He is realizing from hearing the details of the police chief's description, that the garden could well be his own. Finally, there is the fountain in that garden at home.

The merchant is the victim of both robbers and mistaken identity. Historically, people in a down condition often fall into a difficult crowd. They also may experience a loss of energy, followed by a loss of identity, at least temporarily, and a kind of imprisonment.

Now the chief of police has a repetitive dream and there is the strange synchronistic phenomenon of the two men meeting and speaking to each other's situations, at least meaningful for the merchant. The chief of police thinks it is foolish to believe in dreams. But as the tale relates, "the merchant realized at once that the house and garden were his own…[he] uncovered a great treasure…"

The treasure is buried under the fountain. From C.C. G. Jung's *Psychology and Alchemy,* we read…"the fountain in the walled garden [symbolizes] *Constantia in Advensis*—a situation particularly characteristic of alchemy."[2]

Jung writes further: "He thereby protects himself from 'the perils of the soul' that threatened him from without and that attack anyone who is isolated by a secret. The same procedure has also been used since olden times to set a place apart as holy and inviolable."[3]

Jung continues: "The symbolic city as a center of the earth, its four protecting walls laid out in a square: a typical *Tenemos.*"[4]

The tale then reads: "Thus the words of the dream were wondrously fulfilled, and Allah made the ruined merchant rich again." In the context of psychology, we must also relate this image of the merchant story to the archetype of initiation. Jung writes: "One of the commonest dream symbols for this type of release through transcendence is the theme of the lonely journey or pilgrimage, which somehow seems to be a spiritual pilgrimage on which the initiate becomes acquainted with the nature of death. But this is not death as a last judgement or other initiatory trial of strength; it is a journey of release, renunciation, and atonement, presided over and fostered by some spirit of compassion."[5]

Upon reading again the story of "The Dream" just now, I had a few more impressions. A person seems to have to go to a foreign country at times in order to discover treasure back home so that he or she might know what is valuable about his or her home culture, what the true values are, what is praiseworthy about his or her own people. The same could be said about one's inner nature, one's true home in the self. It is the treasure hidden in the garden under the fountain.

If you are depressed or immobilized by shame, you have to connect to the flow of events and people again, even negative ones, so some synchronicity may yet occur. At times of distress, on the level of world events, this may also occur. Those in mediation sessions may become attuned to the uncanny power of the psyche to find a unifying principle for opposites. And some of us may be able to convey this to our leaders.

However, awareness has a leaven-like affect on everyone around. Some people feel these are despairing times in the early years of the twenty-first century. Yet it is possible to talk with people, utilizing a particular consciousness which says, here is another way of viewing things, or this is something you could do about the situation. You will remember that Jung said the world hangs by a single thread, the consciousness of the human being. We must bring that to bear on all the unconsciousness, bigotry, prejudice round us, and in ourselves.

Notes:

1. The Story, "The Dream," Retold by N.J. Dawood, *Aladdin and Other Tales from the Arabian Nights*, London, The Penguin Group, 1996.

2. C. G. Jung, *Psychology and Alchemy*, London, Routledge & Kegan Paul, 1953, p. 166.

3. Ibid., p. 53.

4. Ibid., p. 79.

5. C. G. Jung, *Man and His Symbols*, New York, Doubleday, 1965, pp. 151, 152.

6

Sindbad, Superman and Anxiety

Sindbad the Sailor, in an Arab fairytale, confronts the conflicts which affect all men's lives and which form the bases of anxiety. Portrayed in the imagery of myth, Sindbad's trials speak of patterns which are involved in modern conflicts, although the physical details are different. For more modern physical details, Superman might come to our rescue. However, the two myths, Sindbad and *Superman* the film, in fact, provide some different answers. The psychological subtlety is worth considering; as well, the light which each can throw on creativity as an active power in the confrontation with threat, isolation, and death.

In the episodes from the sixth and seventh voyages, Sindbad confronts one conflict of either sinking into death during the worst circumstances or another process which we shall consider as the heart of imagination in relation to the unconscious as Jung has helped us understand it. There, the link which myth provides is vital for the individual in understanding his spontaneous images as they may speak to his typical confrontation with anxiety.

When we take on such ancient figures as Sindbad we are likely to feel that we are dealing with supernatural myth. How to deal it a death blow with just those words! And yet we are prone to a little fantasy in such works as the film *Superman,* a creation we call science fiction to spare it more harsh treatment, for we accept both the words science and fiction. But, we should remember that science fiction is modern man's fantasy and that *Superman* is one of our fairy tales.

This should give us just that additional amount of tolerance we need to examine other eras of man and other cultures than Western cultures. In doing so, we may discover a common perspective in Sindbad the Sailor from *Tales from the Thousand and One Nights* and our Superman, namely: delight. Delight...and something more, for both show us that man's imagination may triumph and show still a more complete way for man to view himself. Both stories show that a man yearns for what he can not attain in any worldly sense: that is, a power over the human condition. In that respect, Sindbad comes out on top of Superman, but we shall wait till later for that comparison.

What do these two figures have in common? Both are able to fly. Sindbad on a beautiful creature, a great bird called Roc, and Superman, as we know, under his own steam or stream, if you prefer.

Both traverse great spaces. Sindbad's was medieval man's little known space of the great seas; these were the situations of Sindbad's seven voyages. Superman—this modern cinema superman—is cosmic Superman and traverses the galaxies, which is the fantasy (and reality, in part) which has captivated modern man.

Both figures are successful over the aspects of physical harm which usually torture men's minds with fear. Sindbad is subjected to shipwreck at sea, (not a very pleasant thought, although perhaps not so close a danger to modern man) and to many other fates, to which we shall come. Superman, this cosmic one, is of a more dense molecular structure than human beings and therefore not affected by the harms of physical impact from earth objects which so beset modern man: car wrecks, plane crashes, hard blows, etc. But, it is by their specific exploits that we shall know these two figures.

Sindbad is the type of figure who comes close to death time after time. In his seventh voyage, when Sindbad is about to be swept over a waterfall, he resigns himself to death and yields to the flow. As the river catapults him towards the fearful precipice, he silently prays for a merciful end. But as he reaches the very edge, he finds his raft is halted on the water and he himself caught in a net thrown from the bank by a crowd of men.

I must acquaint you a little more with Sindbad. In his sixth journey, he is shipwrecked. His companions who survived, slowly begin to die off one by one on the deserted shore. Finally, Sindbad is the only one left. He digs a grave. He thinks to himself: "When I sense the approach of death I will lie here and die in my grave. In time the wind will bury me with sand."[1]

He wanders off and his eye catches the river which instead of running into the sea disappears into a cavern. He is struck with a plan. "By Allah, he thought, this river must have both a beginning and an end. If it enters the mountain on this side it must surely emerge into daylight again; and if I can but follow its course in some vessel, the current may at last bring me to some inhabited land."[2] He decides to follow this stream. He lashes together a raft and jumps aboard as it becomes caught in the current. His passage is a difficult night passage through an earth chamber, the dark night of the soul, the difficult night journey. This passage gets very tight. His head is right up against the roof. Will it narrow to a point where he can't breath and the inward flow itself becomes strangulated? This is where he goes into a sleeping state: he yields fully to the unconscious powers. When he awakes, his raft is flowing gently on a river through a meadowland under an open sky.

He comes out the other end. No explaining it. The force of the inward running flow takes him to a place he couldn't have known. There was no knowing it without doing it: yielding to the fantasy.

Sindbad admits where he is. In fact he is about to fall into a grave, the worst physical condition we can imagine. Just at this moment, when he accepts where he is—when his mind is free—a new idea breaks in.

Superman is a contrast. When the woman he loves dies, Superman resorts to supernatural power, power even beyond the conditions of his specialness. Here we have two possible options when faced with anxiety producing situations. In Sindbad, it means as one contacts who one is, in that awful moment, one falls into psyche…that means possible movement in one's condition.

What Sindbad achieves in the end is: his life, the humility to shower gifts on Sindbad the Porter, and the overcoming of anxiety. Over and over again, as Sindbad faced each new peril through the story, he would almost give up to the great fear which nearly overcame him and he would for an instant wish despairingly that he had never come on this journey but had remained in the warm comfort of his friends at home. In each instance of near death and a mortifying fear, his eye always seized on something. He was healthy enough and sufficiently childlike to notice something there at hand.

The river which ran inward was not just any river. It was the channel and current of man's capacity to center himself, to find his center, his secret goal, to be himself. What else could quell anxiety? That river—constituted by both the deep cut channel formed over the centuries by man's experience and the flow of life symbolized in movement, e.g. Tai Chi, as man's energized and unified flow, and letting go—created the means to overcome death itself, and the threat of death.

This is why Sindbad is a figure for us. He is like us. He goes on our voyages. He leaves home and comes to a difficult passage. In his heart he wishes that he had never left the safety of the last plateau, the last journey accomplished. But while he is thinking on that and on a fate which will not be reversed, up comes a new perception, which is later wound into a fantasy. The fantasy actually carried to its conclusion, produces a rebirth. Rebirth is the only "out" from death and anxiety.

I connect what Sindbad did with Jung's "active imagination". In the darkest moment, the most terrible moment, Sindbad lets go with his imagination. Something terrible may come up. The only thing to do is to yield to the fantasy. What can happen to a man from his fantasy? Well, something horrifying may come to you through your thoughts. Perhaps this is just one of the reasons which made Jung caution people about using active imagination and urge people to have an experienced guide to work with before setting off on this experiment. Just such a terrifying image marked the fantasy of Sindbad's seventh voyage. Allowing himself to be carried on a current to an unknown interior, Sindbad sensed he might be swept over a waterfall. Carrying on through with this thought meant allowing the psyche to produce its own solution at that moment. Necessarily it will be unknown and unexpected like the net which Sindbad's psyche dreamt or fictionalized over the waterfall. Once he had set out and let go, once he experienced the unconscious process of being hurled towards an unknown end, even death, he could give himself cover to this extent; his fantasy was like a faint of three days incubation which resulted in the symbol which saved him at last and caught him in the net of humanity, so to speak.

After the symbol has happened spontaneously, at the end of this yielding to the unconscious powers, which may indeed wreck one, it becomes our task to see it "as if". As if what, you will ask. As if it were real but knowing it is not, except in a subjective sense. This is why Sindbad the Porter is so vital to Sindbad the Sailor. Sindbad the Porter is the other side of Sindbad the Sailor, his more limited, human side. He could also represent an impoverished point of view, a limited outlook culturally which has come to the end of its usefulness and stands in need of renewal. It is to Sindbad the Porter that Sindbad the Sailor must tell his tales because the Porter is as we are: mortals, persons like you and me. Sindbad the Sailor's tales only tell him how to make of his human condition something more imaginative. In modern jargon, that can cure his anxiety which is the burden Sindbad the Porter carries about his head.

What is this marvelous white dome, because it appears in both Sindbad and Superman? In Sindbad, it is the egg of the giant bird Roc which delivers Sindbad on several occasions. In the film *Superman*, this white dome covers the imperial city of the planet Krypton.

What are we to make of such a large white dome shape which is in fact the egg of a giant bird? What does an egg do? It incubates. It forms itself in the silent and the dark. Where nothing can be seen on the outside, magnificent forces are taking place within. In the darkness of inner brooding a new life is about to take shape. It, too, will be a bird which will leap over the anguish of Sindbad's isolation.

In *Superman*, this white dome is destroyed by the sun of the planet which is close to earth in another galaxy. In the anticipation of that condition the father of cosmic Superman implants a message in the structure of crystal. This message will later become evident to Superman who becomes earth borne.

This is very much like, in imaginary form, the archetypes of Jung which he likens to crystalline structure, simply the abstract structures before any shape has actually taken form. These structures, as we are likely to find them in man's mind, are in his capacity to form an image, e.g. of mother or woman; this image is then conditioned by man's actual experience both of a mother and woman.

What Superman, with all his fantastic qualities, has to communicate to us is that men's and women's minds have within them the capacity to form various images. Like the crystalline structure, these become actualized as we as persons meet the events and the people who activate our sense of being ourselves, of striving, of attaining wholeness as individuals.

When a person discovers these images, many of them powerful enough to wake him or her from sleep or to give him immense peace, he naturally "thinks" like Superman that he comes from another planet, from the heavens. But this is only necessitated because a person can not imagine that his or her mind carries with it the capacity to form images, not so dissimilar to the instincts or Innate Releasing Mechanisms (IRM) which act like instincts and work in the biological level. These inner qualities strike him as coming from the outside, because they are so special he naturally may attribute them to a cosmic source.

This accounts for the whole special appeal of Superman even to minds of rational, scientific, modern man. We know there is something in our natures which can not be wholly accounted for by our experiences. It is the impulse to be more than we are at the present. It is the motive of striving. This inner drive accounts for the inspiration we feel when we hear the Ninth Symphony of Beethoven. We ARE of another world. But that world needn't be regarded as cosmic as modern man is prone to do. That world is the unknown world of our minds which lies behind experience and gives shape to it, to wit the great archetypes of the unconscious.

Now we come to anxiety. In the prologue of the *Tales from the Thousand and One Nights* we have the introduction of that great heroine Shahrazad. She is the teller of the story of Sinbad.

King Shahriyar, having discovered his wife's infidelity, is pale, sick at heart, care-worn and unable to sleep at night, a perfect description of anxiety. His younger brother Shahzaman is also troubled by his wife's orgies and also slays her. He is the famed king who for many days takes a virgin to bed at night and slays her the coming morn. However, it is on him that Shahrazad works; she is versed in wisdom and legends of poets and kings.

The ending of the collection of the *Tales* for Shahzaman is progeny, sleep and love. It is love which has created this the love of his wife, Shahrazad, in place of a destructive sexual attitude. And how has the wife done it?...through imagery, the story. There were, you remember, a thousand and one nights that the stories, or perhaps dreams, went on.

The archetypes of the collective unconscious are the creators of our myths both ancient and modern. They lie behind and within the *Tales from the Thousand and One Nights*, such as Sindbad, and in our modern fiction such as *Superman* and they appear in the dreams of modern people.

Now, let us return from the comparisons of a few aspects of the two stories, to Superman's greatest feat. It is no less than sealing the great San Andreas fault once it has been unsealed and the earth is quaking. This, too, necessitates a journey to the center of the earth. With all Superman's power he must plug up the gap which now exists between the continental plates. This is impossible, we think. It is more planetary and requires powers of a more cosmic nature. Each one of us knows those powers are outside our grasp. There is the near exception of the evil human figures of the film who try to take on unearthly powers themselves. In such a form of unhumanly power these diabolically motivated human figures in the film divert two missiles of the U.S. Navy intended for outer space to the strategic point of the San Andreas fault itself and to a great urban population center. The point comes home. Only the human figures who attain unhuman like power fall prey to diabolical intent. The devil takes over in man's attempt to arrogate unhuman like power to himself.

I had started to say that in my opinion Sindbad was better for us because he represented more of our capacity for transforming our human events by the swift motion of our symbolizing process, imagination and the resources produced spontaneously by the unconscious. Sindbad also has a deep relevance for our current times because of his imaginative, intuitive, open and inclusive attitude. And modern man's imagination, it seems, needs something of more cosmic power, for it is the trajectory of rockets that his mythical heroes must bend. And is it possible that some power lies latent in the unconscious, some imagination of averting war, some super conscious awareness that is great enough to divert man's nuclear trajectory from the planetary destruction which is the source of our deepest and most modern anxiety?

Each one of us must look for that answer within ourselves, within our own capacities for producing imagery. Imagery, according to Jerome Singer of Yale, has come back into its own in psychology after more than fifty years of eclipse. Ironically, it was just in sensory deprivation experiments related to space travel simulation, that man's symbol producing qualities demonstrated themselves irrepressibly.

What it is each of us must simulate with an open mind is a situation like Superman faced with the missiles, which is not unlike our own modern world nuclear dilemma. In the quiet of some morning or the stillness of night, each of us must see those missiles released and hurrying towards some destiny. And we must ask ourselves where they are going and to what ends. Then, like Superman, we must bend them in their course imaginatively until they fulfill SOME higher code on our destiny.

Notes:

1. *Tales from the Thousand and One Nights*, trans. N.J. Dawood, London, Allen Lane, 1977, p. 53.

2. Ibid.

7

Experimentations with Shahrazad

What follows in this chapter is an imaginative piece by a former client of mine. It was inspired in him by the figure Shahrazad. Let us just say that this feminine figure was so powerful for him that it symbolized his whole psychic process during the period of his life conveyed in his story. A Westerner rooted in Western psychology is moved in his inner world by a figure from Tales from the Thousand and One Nights. The text being of an imaginative, creative nature involves a shift to something like the stream of story. For Jung, imagination is psyche. The character Danville experienced healing from this process which he likened to experimentations with Shahrazad. For him, she was like an inner figure which both reflected his experience and got to him through it; hence the title he has given to his story.

In line with our theme of Muslims at the world table, the story tells the impact of an old Arab tale. There is another tie between this modern story and our theme. Jung stated that while the West had developed logos or rational thinking, Arab culture had developed eros. Eros, as relatedness, is here present for the character in this story. It is a place in which we in the West can learn profoundly from Muslim culture. I will give a postscript at the end of the story.

Danville pressed his foot on the accelerator of his Volkswagen. It sped down the tree lined street with ease. The moment felt free, like history would not repeat itself. It was spring alright, and he had to face not getting his sleep, but it would not be like three years ago.

It had all ended very simply. John had walked down to the car with him. Danville had shook his hand in the custom of men. John hadn't said all that much in the analytic session, just that it was time to look out on the day, the sunlit mountains which had appeared in his dreams, and to draw away from the unconscious.

Danville drove now through the four o'clock traffic of suburban Vancouver, through the coastal flats of the Canadian border and back into his native Washington. He felt like going out with his family when he returned home.

◆ ◆ ◆

It was the next day that he decided to jog again. That day, he ran by the ocean-side. And then he walked. The tide was very low. Barnacles dotted all the rocks like tiny porcupines.

"I walked today by the ocean roar…"

He sang out loud: "I walked today where the waves rolled, and the water washed the rocks. I walked today…" He was experimenting, and his voice left the captivity of his lung cage and reached for the sky, where it could be free. He only gave a glance to the railroad tracks above to see if anyone would be watching. His voice was playing. He was moved with his own noise. He was getting into the fun that nature was having around him. Everywhere there was joy.

Danville climbed on down a little further. He wanted to see what the cliffs were like below when the tide was out.

◆ ◆ ◆

Danville was in the caverns. It was past midnight. A man pushed a cart which rattled in the narrow passageway. It reminded him of the scene from movies about Nazis working underground, transporting explosives in the middle of the night. But it was only a basement he was in, and the art contained the linen from the inmates of a progressive mental institution. Danville had been working here for some time. Only now had he been changed to the night shift. It came against his will. It went against his grain. Now he must inhabit the night world of the insane. In the daytime he had the resilience of a small picket fence bracing in the sun. He didn't know if he would be able to sleep in the day time, when he would have his time off—that was the part which concerned him. But as he sat in the quiet of the nursing station he remembered crossings of the English Channel when he had been up at the wee hours of the morning. Now there was something to look forward to. Now, as then, night had brought hours when one was waiting but with no hurry, as one knew that only so, would one reach his destination. In the meantime, one shot the breeze for a little while with the ship's old grand night porter, and then settled into what only the night can bring: freedom of the imagination.

Night porters on the ferries in Europe were a strange breed of men. The closest thing to them in America were the porters on the Pullman coaches when people used to travel across America by train. He remembered in particular one such person. Danville had been in Zurich on business. He had spent some lonely nights there and he had taken the long train trip up the industrial Rhine, calling in innumerable towns. Finally, after riding from the early morning, he reached Hoek Van Holland. It was the English, rather than the Dutch ship going back. The night porter came to his room soon after the ship pulled into the darkness of the night ocean and Europe lay like a necklace on the curl of the ocean sands. "Good Evening, Sir," came the voice of the porter. "May I get a cup of tea?" Had the man just woken up, Danville wondered? What gave him such a sense of being rested and readiness to spend the night as if it were his life? Anyway, he brought that tea. Danville sensed in him a man who had made his peace with his work. He served without a thought. It had entered his nerve framework. Danville felt the grace of this man's union with his "knight of the watch and the crossing". The sheets were very clean. Danville was home again.

◆ ◆ ◆

It was about three o'clock on the next afternoon when Danville woke. Already his family had planned for all to go to the carnival at his daughter's school. When he arrived at the school, his daughter was musing on the balloon she had won. She would let go of the balloon, and it would rise right up to the ceiling. The string would wave a little in the breeze blowing through he building. Jeanine would laugh at the red balloon seeming to wait for her like a dutiful pet.

Now they were in terrible darkness. Danville crawled on his knees holding two large spools of yarn and a red balloon. All he could feel was smooth cardboard underneath him. There was no light. Occasionally he would hear the friendly sound of his daughter laughing up ahead. He was laughing, too. It was "the tunnel". And then he had made several turns inadvertently, he came to what he called "the light at the end of the tunnel".

His wife was downstairs helping with the restaurant which had been set up for the carnival. He saw her, and that vibrant energy of hers reached him. Her doing something unfamiliar like serving hamburgers to lots of people was unusual. And it made her seem like an unfamiliar person. He was drawn to her.

Big and little, young and old they crowded into the next room. Danville stood on the side observing. Soon his eyes caught the table of homemade cakes at the other end of the room. You mean, he quickly thought, you might win one of those cakes for only a five-cent ticket. There was his daughter, Jeanine, and her slightly older sister, Juliette, and her friend. Amongst the four of them they would have a pretty good chance to win. He crowded forward. He knew just where he wanted to join the circle. "The Cake Walk" was nothing more than footprints stuck on the floor with bright numbers on them. Once the music started, he moved forward. When the music stopped he had eloped from "eight", where he had started, to "sixteen". They were drawing the number from the cigar box. "Sixteen". He could hardly believe it. He would have the apricot ripple. Imagine that.

◆ ◆ ◆

Danville drove along in the blackness of an April night. It was 12:30 a.m. The person in the passenger seat spoke in a bare whisper. "So that was what depression was about", she said. She had thought her son and her son's wife were having problems. Perhaps that is why she had left their house while she was still on her home-visit from the hospital. He wondered if this was the case, or was she imagining a situation in her son's life like her own tormented marriage. The woman spoke of hearing "voices" once she had left the son's house.

How had the mind heaped itself up to throw this poor woman there? What a bitter life had been given her after her divorce: sleeping under eaves of industrial buildings when she was pregnant, wanderings. How could the mind, which was capable of producing such beauty in human beings, make into such a creature, a victim of torture?

Danville listened to her account of the last few days when she had been away from the hospital. He knew all too well what she meant when she said that she heard voices. How many Sunday afternoons had he argued with these voices in her. The voices, as the woman would describe them, would say that she should let herself be pulled from a moving car in heavy traffic, by jumping out a back door with her arm caught in the seat belt. Her voice had told her that such a crucifixion was expected of every Christian. Danville had listened to this again and again and had seen the sad look which had come on this woman's face.

When he had first met her, she had the appearance of the woman, the Mary's in Medieval paintings who had surrounded Christ on the cross…that terrible whiteness and grief which was like a prick in each of the upper cheeks which emit dark blood droplets of flagging remorse. She was those tortured medieval would-be Christians which the artists of the time had used for their Mary's.

How horrible to be the victim if such an impulse. Nothing she could do would satisfy such a devouring sprit. It was interested only in death. Danville had pleaded with her waned rational powers, but to no avail. He had fought with the vices until nearly the end of his world. They had eluded him. Only, finally, when he did acknowledge that the woman was spiritual and that her striving was of a spiritual nature, did he really get through to her. He had asked her to paint with chalk paints her heart, which Danville saw as white and square. His vision of her with her friends at the hospital was one with love and caring, and was a way to develop soul and to make it real, he told her.

Now, as they traversed the bleak spaces of the river valley on the way back to the hospital, he heard her say that she had turned herself into a police station when she heard the voices this last time. She hadn't followed them and given her life in crucifixion. Had a guiding spirit intervened? When she told him, this was all he could think of. And he asked her: had a being of the spirit world acted to protect her? She made no answer. In her experience thus far, the only voices and inner personalities had been destructive as far as she seemed to know. It was as though in some awful exchange she had traded the enjoyment of say, smelling a flower, for a crusty crumb from the floor beneath the table.

They arrived back at the hospital. She slept on a couch in the living room that night. Before she had gone to sleep she had smiled up at him through the nurses' station window. She was back home where someone cared for her.

Danville pondered why should we always think that we only belong where there is a blood relationship? Why were we always choosing or attempting to mitigate where we would want to find the love of fellow souls? For when did we not mitigate and instigate, they were there, unbidden.

Danville himself was a man deep in need of love. Danville asked himself, weren't most men and women? With him it was a need to be ignored only with risk to his utter selfhood. When the neurosis had started to crack, he had found himself saying to his analyst, let's be friends. I just want to be friends now, he stated. The perspective person across from him was saying, start believing in yourself, trusting that the friendship is already there.

◆ ◆ ◆

A letter came in the mail after he woke at mid-day. It came from the Jungian analyst with whom he had studied in England.

The analyst wrote: "I certainly found him to be a very sensitive and perceptive person, whose poetic understanding helps him to be in tune with some of the more unconscious processes, both in himself and in his students." Reading the letter, our friend Danville wept. He didn't know why he wept. Perhaps it was because what she said was precisely what he wanted to be.

◆ ◆ ◆

The weeping and the joy wanted to be taken up within his afternoon jog, and soon Danville was on his way. His feet touching the ground and bounding off again, only gave expression to what he felt, coming into his own.

He might want to write something about it, he thought, as he sat on the rocks overlooking the ocean, but he soon just moved toward the rocks. He was squatting on a rock which was normally covered in all but the lowest tides. The waves were just below him. They would rise on the rounded stone on which he sat and sweep over the plants which clung to the rock; the wave would nearly reach him.

He stared into the water and thought of Greece. Greece, too, rises out of the sea, like this place in northern Washington state where he was. It confronts you with music. You hear the cadence of the music which makes you dance. You raise your arms and decide to live. It does all that to you.

In Greece you enter another time. It is not just another history which goes back to antiquity—that is important. It is another sense of time. Westerners want to call the shots. In Greece, TIME calls the shots.

He was thinking of the morning he came to the front desk of his little hotel to ask for directions. No one was there, and he found the proprietor sitting just outside the front door. There he asked about the *Hagia* (or church) in Pronia, the suburb of Toulon. A passer-by heard and said he was going that way. This was his chance. The passer-by wore a bright colored blue shirt. He looked like a sailor. He was smiling, and his mouth showed much gold. He tended to command. Not the sort of person for Danville to pick, but then again Danville hadn't picked him. Sure enough this Greek had worked the docks…in New York.

Just delivering him to the church was not enough, not in a Greek's eyes. He took him inside. The Greek made the American's offering for him. It was essential. He knew the American wouldn't recognize this.

Then there were the paintings on the walls and especially the ceilings. Danville thought of them as paintings. To the Greek man, the figure of John the Apostle seemed like someone he knew. The Greek man only came to the church to revivify his memory of him. These were the things that had happened to Mark, he would say. And Luke, his eyes would open wide and bob in his head. Ah, the baby Jesus, he was oohing and awe struck as if he had been part of the company present in the manger.

Greece could be like that, even for people not so comfortable there as Danville was. He thought of the thousands of tourists in the cafes and the way the Greeks seem to be working on them simply with their spontaneous quality, so that in the end everyone is enjoying things more. Danville remembered the American engineer he had known who was visiting Athens. Of the tourist options available as short trips, the man couldn't decide which he should do. An older friend more knowledgeable of Greece and time, and the unconscious, said to the engineer, why don't you just go down to Constitution Square and have a cup of coffee. While he was down there, a person from his home town in America walked by. He was going to Delphi. Would the engineer like to go along? That was the way things happened in Greece.

Danville often made connections with Greece. The experiences he had there had entered into his soul. He could be returned to them by some swift movement outside his own conscious processes, when bleakness or helplessness called for it. It hadn't been too many weeks before that his patient had been talking of her sorrow. Danville began telling her about how a whole family will sometimes get up and dance in the *taverna*. The patient had later started to think of Greece as having the qualities she had failed to find in Seattle. She would sometimes say, "And in Athens..." Once when Danville was relaxing with a group of patients, and some Greek music came on the radio. When Danville started smiling from a reality he had known in Greece, the patients picked it up immediately. For an instant he had been clairvoyant to his joy. The woman of sorrows had seen it.

◆ ◆ ◆

Danville dropped off to sleep. He woke some four hours later. He was eager to recall what had gone on in the sleep.

He dreamed he was visiting his great-uncle, Douglas. It was very brief. He was in his apartment. The uncle stepped up behind him and said, "Son." Uncle Doug was showing him how he should support himself. Danville was amazed at the dream. I am getting everything I need from the psyche, he thought. Here the psyche was providing that very experience which Danville was lacking. How many times had it come up in Danville's analytic work with his analyst.

It was one of those shifts within the psyche which might be hard to understand to one not familiar with analysis along a Jungian model. Danville had been working the last year on problems related to hurt since his dad had died early.

There was the difficult nature of this relationship with his own son. There was the sense of hurt, which would seem to come up in almost any difficult encounter between himself and another member of the family, especially his wife or son, or both. There was the sadness which seemed to reach into every bone and crevice of his life over the last twenty years.

John, the analyst, had heralded the new note just a few days before when Danville and he had had their session. John, who had first made Danville aware of the source of his pain, spoke to him about a new life stance. It would mean relating to the positive and allowing the positive to fill a void which had been created by its absence over long years. Specifically, John announced that it was time to move from the hurt and sadness. What amazed Danville was that John, in his intuitive way, was to anticipate this development; how analysts could touch that thing which was about to be born. It was like sighting a ship on the seas carrying the most precious and needed cargo, while it was still past the bulge of the horizon. And then again, did recognizing this future possibly and calling it to mind, lend some power to its actual happening?

Danville didn't know the answers to these questions. Anyway he could begin his life again now. The psyche had given its confirmation to the new possibilities which now were positive developments. That suffering as a life-style was over. Someone, a trusted Uncle, had stood behind him in the dream and called him 'son'.

◆ ◆ ◆

Danville watched the two men. It was a filmed version of a story about *Derzu Uzala*, the hunter in Siberia, directed by Kurosawa. Derzu served a Russian captain who was charting the region. The hunter was familiar with the area. In this scene, he and the captain had left the part of soldiers to go and look at a large lake. As they were on their way to the lake, the hunter stopped walking and listening to the wind. He said he was fearful and suggested that the two men return to camp. The captain said he just wanted to go a little further to see the lake. Once they got to the frozen lake, the wind started to blow in a fierce driving motion across the wastes. The hunter was aghast. The wind would obliterate the tracks in the shallow, powdery snow which they had made coming out to the lake. The two set out in some haste to retrace their path to the camp. Almost immediately the footprints were no longer to be found. The hunter would walk quickly searching the ground for some clue as to their route outwards. The men walked rapidly. They would sometimes go for a distance and then find they were cut-off by continuing, by the water. They would go again for a short time in the direction from which they had just come. The hours of the day were wearing on. The men walked hurriedly. They were not in a panic, and yet a wild emotion had begun to enter their feet and walk. Everywhere looked the same. Fatigue was in their footsteps; hurried, anxious motions were there. They had to move fast. After walking some time, they were again cut off from going ahead by the water. They made steps all around in a circle, searching for some clue. The very curved line on their backs suggested that they were experiencing what must have sent terror through man at different intervals throughout his millions of years of existence. They were lost. Danville, working as he did, now knew what his schizophrenic patients must experience and feel, a kind of lostness. He wanted to help them. And yet each one of his patients would take a kind of spendthrift love which was beyond his, or probably anyone's, reach. He could give but a measure each day.

Derzu got himself and his civilized companion through the Siberian desolate space—the winds and bitter cold of that night by cutting the dry grass and building a shelter with it. The two were able to carry on.

Derzu knew almost everything, it seemed, about the forests. He had lived there many years simply by trapping and hunting. If nature was put out of Tao by bad men, Derzu would set it right for example by destroying the traps which had been left in place by careless men after abandoning an area. Derzu could tell the footprints of an old man. The exploring party came across one such person, a Chinese man in the midst of a patch of trees. Derzu was familiar with this individual. The Captain, out of kindness, offered the Chinese a thick soup and a cup of hot drink. Although he at first refused, the Chinese did take these. Later in the evening, the Captain suggested that Derzu get the Chinese man, who sat by himself some distance away, to come and share their fire. "Don't trouble him; leave him to his dreams; he is dreaming of his house in China; it is springtime and the trees are in blossom," Derzu said. "The Chinese had left home when his brother stole his wife. He has been wandering in the forests for forty years." Danville watched. Again he saw his patients, unrecovered from blows to the very trunks of the life processes. How many were just like this hermit; timid and isolated in their remorse and loss?

◆ ◆ ◆

Danville once had a dream where he was sitting in this big banquet-type room, filled with people. Nothing was yet happening. A couple came by, and Danville's wife decided to give her seat to the woman, who had a baby in her arms. Would his wife sit by him on the small fold-up wooden chair? Danville thought. Or would he, too, rise? He got up. Soon he was going around the edge of the hall, and his movements seemed to coincide with a deep, walking cadence of music which filled the room. This seemed to get everything started. While seated he had spotted the arrival of a beautiful woman with black hair and blue eyes who sat down by the door. As Danville passed around the edges of the room, people took partners. He didn't take anyone yet, and his action made him curious and aware of himself. He passed this woman who had arrived, and greeted her. Others had made choices, and now almost everyone was paired up. They began the song, "Let me call you Sweetheart." He would be able to join in, on the second dance.

Danville woke from the dream. He knew it was a special one. Later he laid on his belly looking out across the bay. The bright sun shone on the snow covered mountains beyond. Danville captured the dream, writing it in his collection of papers. A certain feeling came from the dream. He wrote:

"It is the period of the first true happiness I have experienced in my life. It comes when I have had to face something unpleasant and a challenge." It was unpleasant for him to work nights. It was a challenge to face it as such. Once he discovered that the change was working out, the challenge became to not cling to feelings of being wronged. Rather, it was to accept that he had received, in spite of everything, or even because of the difficulties, as he first had seen them. This brought the realization that it is an ultimate quality of selfishness when one has received very positive things from a difficult situation, to continue in one's framework of disappointment and hurt.

The whole scene of his psyche was moving now like the dancers on the floor. Through rising to the changed situation of no longer having two seats with his wife, he found that he was giving off some energy which had the effect of getting the whole group moving and paired into dancing couples. What about himself? In the dream he didn't have a partner. He wasn't going to worry and let that affect his feeling of wonder about the dream. He suspected his situation would be redressed in a future dream.

That happened to follow. In this dream he was waiting. It was an apartment, but there was a large space. A young woman was there. He told her how beautiful her bosom was, as she lay on her side. She was completely unselfconscious. There was a birthmark on the side of her chest (like his, he thought). When she was up on the floor, he suggested dancing with her. He took off his under shorts as well. He held back any premature flow. They were dancing together.

This dream filled him with a sense of wonder, and joyfulness. It was like the joyfulness one might have experienced in early sex. It was like the figure, completely natural. The figure was a little like a dancer he had known once who was herself completely natural. It would be ridiculous to think this dream meant that person, as a person. The woman of the dream had the same birthmark on her chest as he did. She could be none other than the feminine side of himself, who came to birth when he did. She was his "psyche" or soul. He was at home with himself, and with her.

◆ ◆ ◆

Danville was jogging along the lake. He hadn't come there in a while. He wondered at the fact that his right foot no longer hurt. It has been several months now since he had been able to run on it. He tried to find soft earth on the verges of the path. His feet dearly loved the earth where it was natural and had not been packed down. It seemed as if there were a pact between feet and earth, as though they belonged to one another. He felt a spring in his run. When he was running he tried to let problems escape from his mind. He knew how petty the ego could be, counting everything up, being sensitive to every possible remark by others.

Danville was really feeling good. The lake was neither happy nor sad today. There wasn't any brilliant blue sun, nor any heavy overcast. He came upon the portions where the path made a swift flight over the hill; he coasted letting his arms fling out and rattle around. For a second he was concerned about a new friend of his daughter's who always seemed to be eating at his house. And then he gave himself back over to running. He felt his foot ache just a little. *I want to reach the end of this side of the lake*, he thought to himself. It was a strong urge, but immediately he stopped. He laughed to himself. He loved his foot. He said to it in effect, okay, you need to stop. It was a part of him. He liked the feeling of looking at his foot in this way. He knew it was like seeing the whole of his body as a community of parts.

His mind turned now to the image of his foot. It was healing. But it was not completely well. It kept him from "flooring" it. It also gave him the painful, yet accurate, picture that he was not fully well. He would have been really irritated with this in the past, even threatened. *What? His body was not perfectly at his command?* He smiled: he could see a little Nazi up there in the control tower shouting signals. But the easing off at this moment gave Danville such a pleasurable sense. No need to be a heel about it. Healing was in his interest. The awareness of the healing of his psyche which started taking place some three years back, was the force which bound up his life into a whole. In fact to heal meant to make whole. At least the healing events of his life explained all the things which were important to him now; his own dreams, his work with patients, his love of his wife. Even his jogging and his love of nature were intimately tied in with healing and living in the direction of wholeness.

So many things had happened to him. He felt inspired when he thought about them.

◆ ◆ ◆

Whitman Sanger sat in front of him. A man whose smile could not be contained. Danville felt the sheer pleasure of being with an old friend. Whitman was visiting from out of town.

The two old friends were comfortable in the wee hours of the morning. The night breeze sent it's eternal quality through the room and the psyche.

Danville said his mind was roaming past "breeze" to the breezes of Epidauros.

"When we were there," Whitman said, "we only attended the performances of ancient drama which were given in the amphitheater. That was cathartic enough for me to know what you are talking about."

"When we came to the heart of the precinct," Danville continued, "several things were taking place. The statue of the God of healing, Asklepios was there. Whitman, I saw the old 'guy' there. And I just felt like going up to him. If people of old asked for healing, might not I? I can't tell you why or how, but I just did. Maybe it was a little bit of magic. Or maybe in that moment I was just letting my heart's wish speak."

"The rest was a little complicated," Danville said. "I noticed that Sabina was roaming around with her guidebook in her hand and a perplexed look on her face. She was unhappy not to be able to locate the porch where those who came to ancient site slept. She was so intent. Seeing her work like this, searching for the prime spot, I knew why we were together. Well, you know what wonderful qualities she has. But, looking as she was for this, I knew why we were married. That as a great discovery and a great thrill, as you might imagine."

"We were soon satisfied that we had found the porch," Danville added. "After making their offerings to Asklepios, the God of healing, those afflicted then came here. Under a roof supported by a long series of columns, the afflicted slept. Do you know what they were waiting on? It was here in this spot that they hoped, while they slept to have a healing dream."

"Oh?" Whitman now almost hummed.

"Yes," Danville continued, "those who slept on the porch did so expectantly. They hoped for the appearance of Asklepios. It was reputed that he did so for the afflicted pilgrims and in the dream he would tell them the substance of action they needed for healing."

"There are a few things I have to tell you about," said Danville. "First, Sabina and I together found the place where they drew their water. There was a cleft in the ground lined with stone and going down about forty feet. We also saw bits of pottery still in the earth there. In both things we seemed very close to the articles of the people who came there in ancient times. But, in the well especially I felt I dwelled in the time of this ancient shrine, itself."

"I had to find the entrance," Danville said, "because we hadn't come by that way. Then I returned to the place where the main building had been. Sabina was still combing the area, and I sat again near the shrine of Asklepios. I was just resting. Then it came to me: I could be an analyst! You know, Whitman, that is what I've always wanted to do."

Whitman and Danville continued talking for some time. Danville asked if he too, experienced such times of healing?

"My life has had such a different pattern," Whitman said. "It seems I have had to find out about life through relationships. After Ramona and I broke up, and I had Seth part of the time, I started dating again. Maria and I were intensely in love for a long time there. She was very taken with my art. She would try to help so much when I was writing, and my love for her inspired an intense new phase in my poetry. But with Seth's terrible fall on that picnic, I felt I had to exclude all other things until he was well."

Danville propped his head up with his arm. Then he reached for the back of his neck and rubbed it.

"You just need some sleep," Whitman suggested.

"Yes, I guess I am getting a bit tired," Danville admitted. The two friends rose and clasped each others' shoulders.

"G'night, Whit."

"Sweet dreams!"

◆ ◆ ◆

It was 2:00 a.m., and Danville felt he had cause to write in his diary. It had been an incredible meeting with John, and only now did he have time to get back to those events. It had begun when Danville had reported a dream. In the dream, he was speaking with a woman, one who had been married to another of his uncles, and later divorced from him before his tragic death. Danville said to her, "You know Ron was good at sports; Rich, his brother, was as well. They made it to the state finals in basketball. Then there was Will, my first cousin…" Then Danville was weeping. He put the newspaper up in front of his face.

While this dream amazed Danville, he felt all day as if his tear ducts had received tremendous exercise. Yes, he had tried to look for the positive instead of his own suffering in the last few weeks, but this weeping was inscrutable.

John invited Danville, his analysand, to actively use his imagination to find this weeping. Although Danville had had many years of working on his dreams, he found that some things eluded him. This weeping was like that. Even before Danville arrived at John's, he had thought of taking to the couch to let his mind go more free. As the hour which Danville and John had together neared its appointed end, Danville laid back on the couch. "I am weeping because I haven't succeeded like the men on that side of the family," he said. John was listening. Danville's mind went deeper. "My mother," he said, "loved this brother of hers who died. She helped raise him. She felt how he had been cut off in the prime of his life, and this was almost more than she could cope with, especially with my father's own untimely death."

Finally, Danville found himself saying: "I am really like her. When I was growing up, that was my nature. Simple, sweet-natured, and generous. At about twenty-five I don't know what happened, but I lost all of that, and I became critical."

What did it mean that Danville discovered his connection to his mother's personality in this way? He couldn't get over it, how he wanted to say how he used to be, how his personality had been then…He let his mind wander. "My heart is broken." He wondered what this could mean. Who was hurt? He could reach back to an individual who was very different by nature than he was today. In all his dealings with people then, he didn't have to act as he did as a matter of course today. He couldn't get over the difference. He remembered the world at college and New York being cold. Now he seemed only to care that no one climbed his fence. He thought now he could be good to his "heart" again.

Being a Christian in those years, Danville suffered. Wasn't Jesus, in the fulfillment of the Isaah's prophesies, "a man of sorrows, acquainted with grief"? Wasn't Jesus a figure on the cross, he thought in those days. To contrast this in his present way of being, he could only think how he once had felt when he was listening to the hymn being played by an ensemble and chorus, "Oh Sacred head now wounded." He remembered weeping.

Was his crying in the dream any different? The grief of his mother which she felt for a husband and then a brother cut off in the prime of his life, as a human grief, on a human level. That was the difference. He felt grief for HER, and like hers. His caring took him into a deep connection with a quality basic in him and transformative of those years of critical relation to others.

◆ ◆ ◆

The next day Danville woke from his sleep in the afternoon. He took off the sleep mask which shut out the daylight and its stimulation to his system. His dreams still hovered over his bed. "Don't get too much into the day, yet," his mind thought. Slowly the dreams seeped into the cup of his conscious memory. There, first imagine: warmth. Only with warmth, could one substance reach another to make a vital transfer of image and message. Yes, after a positive outlook, warmth was the thing needed.

How had he missed this? It seemed his consciousness had over looked it. Only a day earlier he had uncovered the fact that his personality used to be like his mother's: kind, trusting and generous. Such a revolutionary discovery, something to possibly build a whole new approach to himself. And today, he thought, the dream had come up with still another approach, another basic potential personality change. My dreams, he thought, keep marching on.

Danville woke. Danville had this sense of the psyche providing what he needed. "There is an afterlife," it was clear to him after the dream, in an intuitive leap. "The soul goes on after death. How else do we explain it that the psychic life of a person attains so much?"

His burning question, as it was a week prior to this event, was: how could this whole dream in which the human being understands so much about nature, end? Now the answer had come.

◆ ◆ ◆

Danville had dreamed of Mohammed Ali, the boxer. He got things done through having a strong fist, by which he could put down any opponents. His was the way of being the strongest physically. He had a little jingle in which he described himself as being able to inflict a sting after tricking his opponent. He was light like a butterfly, but able to sting like a bee. As much as anything else, the tune and the poetry were mesmerizing. Was that his secret? Did he know how, through a combination of sounds and rhythms, to disarm an opponent? In other words, was he an arch manipulator? He was stronger than me—that was the point, thought Danville.

Danville wouldn't like to meet him in a fight even if it were only a benefit. Why one small blow from that guy could put him out right away. You see, Mohammed Ali was Danville's shadow. He personified what was unconscious in Dan's personality. Danville knew that. In the dream of such a figure he could recognize something opposite to his personality as he had established it. He knew now. Even as Mohammad Ali would say (albeit as a crying protest), "I am the greatest," Danville knew this was the quality which he was lacking in himself. He, Danville, was more likely to carry a placard stating: "I am the littlest." That grew out of his early religious experience, because, in that way of thinking, only God was great. It was a dangerous way to get started off in life. It probably accounted for his over interest in the unconscious, in things psychic.

For Danville, his qualities of being both light with language and rhythmic were still in the power of a superiority/inferiority complex. His language was for him still an effort to be above others. Meanwhile, his own physical strength and presence were buried, remained in control of his unconscious. The fact that this quality was mostly below awareness because it left him walking around entitled "the littlest." It also meant others, and himself, could be menaced by a power which was not conscious and subject to his daylight values. Any person who had been the victim of the sting of his words knew that.

Danville knew he could not win over the greater fighter. He had to use his wit. Why not invite the fighter to be in a play. They could entertain the others in this way. He could let the great fighter chase him around the room, and could do stunts with trays and cups. The one thing he must not do was use what was his family treasury. The latter must not be mocked or misused.

In the dream, the great fighter agreed. That showed a stepping stone toward a different relationship to aspects of himself. Instead of having physical control over himself and others, the big strength could expend itself entertaining others. Danville could catch up the big guy through a plot to humor him and others, and win over a menacing part of himself.

◆ ◆ ◆

Danville wakened at about one o'clock in the afternoon. He didn't mind sleeping only four hours after his night shift. Secretly, he couldn't wait to see if the house was empty or if any of his family were around for Saturday. He peeped through the glass door into the kitchen, and his heart gladdened. There were his wife, son and daughter.

"Dad," his son said, "could we go down to the bay and do some sketching?"

"Sure, Kerry." He knew his wife had been waiting to see him, but he also knew she would be pleased he could be with his son in this way.

The two joined up a little past the railroad bridge which went across the small sea inlet. Kerry didn't want to jog, but Danville wanted to work it in. It always made him feel free, to run. Today, as many other days, as his feet bounded upon the thick grass, he felt like a native of the forest.

"Dad, how much money will you make when you are an analyst?"

"Analysts make about forty dollars an hour."

"That's not too much. But how much would you make in a year?"

"I wouldn't be working eight hours a day, five days a week. I would probably work more like five hours a day, four days a week. As an analyst, you have to have time to keep centered, or else you can't do your work. It's like an artist; as you know, you can't work all the time; you need sometime to replenish yourself."

"What does an analyst do?"

"He helps people with their problems. Not only that, maybe the client gets off on the wrong track and has to find a way back."

"Dad, could we go up there?" Kerry pointed to a steep slide of earth which rose above the railroad tracks. Danville scurried along behind him. His son had always asked certain kinds of favors. This was one type: will you follow me you-know-where? Danville was compliant. He only asked the small sapling there if they would forgive him pulling on them—it was them or him!

They sat down to sketch on a perch of mountain high above the sea, looking out to the large bay. It was perfect. What to draw? A rock called for Danville to straddle it. In front of him was a branch of wild dogwood. Danville couldn't get over the beauty of its graceful line curving upward. He had to draw it before everything else, even the wild beauty of the sea expanse.

"An ant is chasing us. It has even called its friends."

"That's imagination working," Danville said to his son. "There's nothing wrong with it. It's just that it doesn't work in every field. You are not food."

Before Danville could say anything more, Kerry was off on the next path.

◆ ◆ ◆

The two of them lay on the floor of the den. Whitman had his hand cupped by his ear as if to take in something fresh and also to move toward the stereo speaker and away from the noise, being made by Dan's children in the other room. Danville lay by the other speaker. It was a radio program on the life of Jung.

Although Whitman was one of Danville's closest friends and Danville didn't get to see him often, Danville suggested that the two listen to this program. For a flicker, Danville had wondered about this, but hadn't let it concern him further. Now the body pose of Whitman, itself, showed what was being reacted to. Moreover, there was a history.

What was so remarkable about the program that it drew the two men to it? Indeed, what was the connection between the individuated Jung and these two men in their early forties?

Their own friendship had begun in college stage production. Whitman, with his twinkle in his eye, had played a magician. Always that power had played into his being. Danville remembered him in a scene flying. That, too, seemed a residual part of Whitman's make-up, at least up to the point of their present meeting.

It was probable that Whitman had been in love with Sabina for a time, but he had loved many women. That was akin to his deep need and ability to feel. Unlike most people who hide their emotions and feelings of love and caring, Whitman lived and articulated his. This led to a rich and powerful emotional life, and one in which many women were involved.

Momentous events in their personal lives had connected these two men. Danville was able to bring into life something in himself with Whitman during the free life of college. At its peak in college, this freedom to be in the feeling realm had given Danville deep satisfaction. There was another such person in their company then. He was Puerto Rican. His name was Rico. His small stubby hands held warmth as he grasped the hands of others to convey caring. His eyes often nearly watered in a way which seemed to carry the other individual within a sense of loyalty and togetherness. There were happy times with the three. All dabbled with art. Rico painted and wrote poems. Whitman tried his hand at long poetic pieces. And Danville dared sometimes to write a few lines of free verse.

All was well in those university days. Danville married Sabina. Rico and Whitman were there to share the glories of the wedding event. In the image of youth, life seemed to be moving toward yet a more perfect fulfillment.

But it didn't work that way. Danville and Sabina tried their luck and gamed for experience in the vast world of New York City, leaving behind them the simple pleasures of the New Mexico skies and its outdoor warmth. Rico eventually came to New York, too. Whitman stayed with the Southwest.

Some years went by. Danville was preoccupied with his work and his new family. Whitman had begun to make a place for himself. He now had an apartment and advanced in his work. Later Whitman and a young woman from Queens were married. They created quite a nice apartment together, and Whitman again showed his creativity. Many friends came to their home for parties and dinner. Often they got together friends for poetry readings. Always, these times were events for those who came. Danville and Sabina again found the pleasure of their old friend's company.

There was another event which would always be remembered by the friends. Whitman and his wife returned from a holiday in Greece. And they came to visit Danville and Sabina. It was a very free moment. The two couples were sitting on the floor of Danville's Long Island house. Whitman began describing being in Delphi, a place of special importance to Danville. Whitman and Nora said that they conceived a child there.

Danville was very moved by this, so much so that he had to go to his room, where he sat on the bed and wrote:

> They stole away to Delphi. The couple stayed
> where rocks are reaching out to touch the air
> and gods would play if gods did anywhere.
> Their bed on the lip of infinity was laid,
> and drunk with sky, they clove to mortal frame.
> In such a old a civilization could fair
> forth; in such a fold our earthly pair
> conceived a child above the olive plain.
> Lie peaceful little babe in mother's fold.
> Then later when down lies dark upon your face
> and stones are dreamt like those, may you be told—
> should you be led, this reliquary to trace,
> they stole away to Delphi. What vapors rolled,
> what tales of destiny in this moment of embrace.

Events in Whitman's discovery of himself now led him to return to New Mexico with his wife from New York. Danville and Sabina, themselves, soon departed from New York to live in England. But always Whitman and Danville were close.

Whitman often felt compelled to write his old friend as moments of special strength occurred in his life. Often the letters overflowed into poetry.

When Danville and Sabina returned to America and Danville was going for an interview for a job he wanted at a mental hospital, he stopped at a coffee shop just before his appointment. So much rested on the outcome. He remembered pausing for a moment and clearing his mind. Then the image of his old friend came together with that of his great-uncle. They gave him that pleasure and confidence which transcended worries and a mere daily perspective on life. The image of his Uncle Douglas connected him with his ordinary background of growing up in a small coal-mining town. There was pride and dignity in this way of life which so contrasted to the famous people he met. Likewise, the image of Whitman suggested the humble rather than the elite. Danville got the job.

These were some of the connections between the two men which went through Danville's mind as the two listened to the radio. Whitman was later to write:

"A man gathers in one spirit
the effort of living a life
cast in one's own unique mold,
yielding ever to what it means
to be 'me' and none other,
The two friends gather in one spirit
afflicted once, and effect
lives smoldering on fires of the creative new
saying yes to the deepest sigh between friends
and hearing a deep bell, unfathomable."

◆ ◆ ◆

"Hello, Dan."

"Hello, Whit."

"How was the night?"

"Alright."

Danville unloaded his things and noted that his daughters were getting their breakfast.

"What kind of breakfast would you like this morning, Whit?"

"What you cooked yesterday was just fine."

"Oh, let's have something more interesting. I could do scrambled eggs or French toast. Which would you prefer?"

"Well, French toast."

Soon the girls were on their way to school, and the two men had sat down to the breakfast meal. Whitman broke the silence: "I can feel your energy going down, down," he interjected.

"You're right, I'm tuning down." Danville thought of being in bed in fifteen minutes, something he had looked forward to all during the night shift.

"You haven't said much about where you are since I've been here. I hope we get a chance to talk about it before I go back," Whitman said softly.

Danville felt himself wake up a little. Had anyone asked him that in years, he wondered to himself. Okay, he thought:

"When we listened to the program on Jung together the other night, it brought up in me several things I want to do. What the program was able to make me feel 'the courage to be', my own individuality."

"Me, too, Danville."

"I can tell you about what I want to do. I want to carry forward with this dream to be an analyst. I want to work with the schizophrenic patients at the hospital. And I would like to develop a way of speaking to other people in our study group on holistic healing, to make real the psyche. I'm sure some of them live with it, but I don't find many people who can put that experience into words. I want to do that with them."

All of a sudden Danville had the courage to say what he had only been able to say in a short poem two nights before. "When I watched you the other night, I found a calm and certitude; that is a great achievement. I know how much pain you have had. I felt that strength in you. It was like a platform of consciousness about right here." Danville pointed to his heart. He had articulated what was important in his feelings. He went off to bed feeling tired but fully charged and fully himself.

◆ ◆ ◆

When Danville woke in the afternoon, he hadn't had a single dream. Whitman, the house guest, was not downstairs. Danville drank his cup of milk with a spoon of honey stirred in it, and went off for his run by the sea. When he got back, Whitman and Danville's daughter Jeanine were busy preparing supper. Danville put on his favorite record from Greece. It was the music of Hadjidakis, using mostly the *bouzouki*. Danville had come from the shower with only a pair of trousers on. Once the music had started he could no longer make his way upstairs to dress. He began dancing. His arms raised above his head like "Zorba" complete with the joy of having a close friend there for supper.

He felt the sensuousness of his unclothed chest, and yet he longed for no other. His feet bounced from the floor in the strenuous steps of the Greek dance. At first he wondered if he would tire, then an image came to mind. He was thinking of the lovely, light foot of the barefoot woman he had seen with her daughter the night before.

The foot had been tapping and bounding as his foot. He was dancing that foot's beauty. He did not tire.

Tasso came to Danville's mind. In the small town of Toulon on the Peloponesos, Danville would wake from his afternoon nap. His mind would head for the near-by hotel, walk past the tight concierge and into the small bar with its cold marble floor. He would be the only person in the room. And Tasso, the waiter, would bring him Greek coffee. They would walk. Tasso, who played the *bouzouki*, would say he had not slept again the past night. Each night this smiling, short, stocky young man, would go with his friends to play music. Neither Tasso nor Danville could speak much of the other's language. And yet they always managed to talk. Danville would get a completely electric feeling by being near the artist. He would then sit in the corner and work on his writings concerning Shahrazad and the *Tales from the Thousand and One Nights,* utterly content. Now, in his experience the inner meaning of those tales were coming back to him on still another level. Was it not Shahrazad's stories which had tamed the night world of the insane? Had not his own recording of the story during this period of working the night shift in the mental hospital, tamed this experience for him?

◆ ◆ ◆

In the dream of that evening, Danville said: "I was in my quiet, spacious house located in the town where I work. My boss came to visit me in the evening. He and the head nurse from the mental hospital sat down at the kitchen table. I couldn't imagine why they were there, except perhaps to tell me that my dream of becoming a psychologist was, or perhaps wasn't, going to come true. The boss wandered off into the living room and the nurse kept talking but I didn't know about what. Another figure came into the living room. He was a big black man with broad cheek bones, a jazz musician. I greeted him. He entered into the small room. Then I went toward the living room. I passed my son who was sleeping on a small hide-a-bed couch. He was alright. And I felt a lot of love for him. Once I reached the living room, there smiling full-faced with a broad brown hat on, was a minister I met when I first came to this town. His face was so loving and complete. He was sitting behind a small round coffee table."

◆ ◆ ◆

Danville woke. He recognized the self, to use Jung's terms. It portended a development in Danville.

The self was no longer menacing. It was the symbol, according to Jung, of the widest, most complete development of the psyche. It was imperishable. As a potentiality in Danville, it had to do with the realization of his totality. That image of wholeness was what had originally attracted him to Jung.

When Whitman had asked Danville about what was transpiring in his life, Danville had given part of the answer by saying what he had felt when he had heard the program on Jung. There was more, he just didn't know how to tell him about the rest. It had begun some three years before. Danville had lost work which was meaningful to him in counseling students and coaching them along the lines of their deepest interests, toward career development. When he hadn't been able to find other work in England where he was living at the time, he made a trip back to America to seek employment. Having been gone for five years, Danville was subjected to a rude shock: having no current position or residence in the U.S., he had lost a foothold from which to gain a new position.

◆ ◆ ◆

Later Danville decided to try to tell Whitman about these experiences of an inner nature. He said simply: "You know when I returned to America three years ago in order to get a job and relocate here, I ran into some troubles almost immediately. First of all there was the time change. My friends in Boston were just going to bed when I felt that burst of energy I get early in the morning. I couldn't sleep. Well, that was one thing. The thing was, it didn't just last the first few days, or even the first week. In fact, I hardly slept the whole five weeks I was here. When I got back to England, there was no relenting in the situation. By then I was beginning to drag around. I felt miserable. What to do? I would wake up after just a few hours sleep at the beginning of the night, and then I would not be able to go back to sleep. My dreams were upsetting. I remember one in which the life of my child, Jeanine, was threatened. Then I knew I was on the wrong track wanting to return to America to a job that was not in my main field of psychology and therapy. I got a real shock from that and changed my direction. I would not, I decided, do anything which would threaten her. She was one of the most important things in the world to me. But you see she wasn't just my daughter she was also me. The dream had chosen this image to represent my own young soul. This brought me back to my deep interest in psychology, even though I had no way to earn my living with it at the moment. When I say psychology I mean the kind which deals with inner experiences or that of the soul."

"It was about this time," Danville continued, "that I discovered the *Tales from the Thousand and One Nights.* I don't know if you are familiar with it or not."

"Isn't it the story of Shahrazad?"

"Yes, Whit, exactly. Shahrazad was my story so to speak, though of course not in details. Do you remember how it went?"

"Well, yes. It seems this king went off on a terrible tangent when he discovered his wife was being unfaithful to him. He killed her. Then each night, he took a new bride, and the following day he had her executed."

"Right, Whit. When Shahrazad met him he was in a terrible plight. If we look at his psychologically, we would have to say, the king had no relationship with his inner experience, his feelings. He was continually cutting himself off from this. The story says he was pale and without sleep. The parallel to me was that I had not been faithful to my feelings at that time. But the important point was this. Do you remember how the king got healed?"

Whit nodded, "Go ahead."

"Shahrazad developed this ploy. She would become the King's bride. She would tell him stories before he returned at night. Thus it went on, for a thousand and one nights, when, as the book relates, the king honored Shahrazad for giving him a progeny, dreams and sleep. The woman in the story had connected the king to his own vital inner process; she was that process. And her stories were like his dreams or imagination."

"I see," said Whit.

"For me," said Danville, "the stories brought by my dreams also brought me progeny—in my case, sweet relations with them, dreams and sleep."

◆ ◆ ◆

Danville was sitting across from his wife at the supper table. The dishes were still there but the children had already risen and left for more active sport.

"If you were twenty-one again," Sabina was asking, "and you knew what you know now, would you live your life any differently?"

"I would. I would be simple, good natured and generous. These were the foundations of my life in my early years, and I would live them again."

Sabina looked bowled over. She didn't say anything but she was amazed. What happened to transform this man?

Danville could see her wonder and her happiness. In his heart of hearts he knew. Those dark years had been worked through. Instead of seeing the things he didn't like about himself, as projected on others, he had owned up to them. It had taken some years. But it had left him free to turn and see, as his dream had shown, the sun upon the mountains.

Danville did one more thing before he went to bed that night. He went to his son's room and he read him his dreams. In those dreams Danville passed by his son sleeping on a cot. Danville realized he was alright, and he loved him very much. Both males slept that night as they never had done before.

The dream had come true. Like the husband of Shahrazad he had after a thousand and one nights, been healed.

POST-SCRIPT TO CHAPTER SEVEN

We have journeyed in many ways through *Tales from the Thousand and One Nights*. Now I can return to the words soul, psyche, anima, and add one further definition of self. These are words, values and realities which I believe the West shares with Muslim culture.

Soul, psyche and anima are the same word deriving respectively from English, Greek and Latin. I shall give some different innuendoes for our purposes to these forms of this basic word.

Soul is the felt experience of one's innermost being. Soul is emphasized in some forms of Jungian psychology such as Archetypal Psychology, and represents a way of seeing into experience and reflecting on it, one sees, listens to how the inner being is effected and moved, more so than other considerations such as practical ones, problem solving, etc. Danville, I believe, was doing the work of soul, conceived in the image of experimentations with Shahrazad.

Anima is the contrasexual quality in a man, and more. As Jung suggested, it may represent the female genetic presence in his body. It is also responsible for moods, vague hunches, etc. It mediates the unconscious. The contrasexual part in a woman is called *animus* and represents the inner spirit. The anima exists for both men and women. The anima needs to be seen also as beyond the individual and connected with the world soul. Shahrazad could be seen as an anima figure as well as the other feminine figures in Danville's dream.

Psyche as I have said, is another word for soul. However, in our usage, it also implies the unconscious, or collective unconscious, or better the objective psyche. It is the matrix for ego and consciousness, and from its depths and reality all judgments are made. Its limits, like consciousness, are unknown and may merge with the world e.g., as world soul. The Jungian view is that when one like Danville enters the world of psyche, the imagined world, then healing can come. The *Tales from the Thousand and One Nights* are the healing workings of psyche.

The psyche meets me anytime I feel, anytime an event touches my heart. That event can be inner or outer. When I care deeply about another person, then I am with psyche. When I am moved by suffering, my own or others, then that is psyche. Perhaps I may be moved by a sudden recognition of my own true form, witnessed in a moment of deep communion with another person, a client…or other events in which I sit by the stream of life. I may hear the roar of water, feel the freshness of the air, and know that I am, but also know that I move in some deeper dimension of life. Then I am with psyche. Too, when I am aware to my own death and close to it in feeling, then the life-quality of psyche is known. Whatever the problems of the moment if I may be so lucky to see them reflected in the images of archetypes or in some way contact the collective psyche under me, then I realize that all is not lost. Rather I am filled with a sense of nobility about my condition; it is connected to the deep in life and in all time.

The self is a reality experienced as the symbol of the totality of human experience and the unification of all opposites, such as masculine/feminine, conscious/unconscious, logos/eros. In dreams and world art, it often is represented as a circle divided into four parts or a variation of four parts. It is the motivating factor and the image of becoming whole. Jung has called it the God-image in the human being. If it is not heeded, it can become destructive. Danville's life starts to line up with it, so to speak.

Eros was defined by one of my teachers, M. Esther Harding, as relatedness. Eros is contrasted with logos. Eros is a quality which has been more associated with the feminine, in the sense that Dr. Harding was using it. We have already seen how Jung felt this quality has been very developed in Arab culture. We have seen, too, how King Shahriyar was transformed by psyche and by Eros.

To follow logos is to be guided by principles, research facts and their logical interconnections. This is the dominant viewpoint of the Western world. To follow eros is to, at times, yield some non-eros consideration in favor of the connection to another, very real human being, in spite of the experience of anomalies, imperfections, compromise, ambiguity, and inner conflict.

The feminine principle, again as Esther Harding points out, is seeing with the light of the moon as contrasted to seeing with the light of the sun. The moon's light is more diffuse than the sun's. The moon is the light of the night. The moon vision symbolizes seeing in the nightness of things, their partial darkness, hiddenness, unconsciousness. Hence, the feminine principles is seeing and understanding where there is more ambiguity and unconsciousness, and less clearly defined outlines than the conscious daytime, sun-lit world. In all the great world's religions there is a special place for Wisdom in the form of the feminine.

I recall an experience with a group of women. There was something important happening in the group that night. I think I was experiencing the feminine as the women talked with one another. I saw how refined they were, how they had taken various ideas of development, psychological and spiritual, and applied these to themselves. I saw how they cared, as do I, about the personal dynamics involved in situations. When a slight was brought to their attention they responded with communication and feeling. This feminine was present in me as a male. I seem to be very at home in groups of women. I imagine this would be a great contrast to the life which one of my friends has had. I know his dad would not have respected spending time in groups of women, and this was a great oversight on his part. I know it has been the most important thing for me to be there where the dynamics of human communication and the inner feelings of a person could be brought out more, respected and rewarded in all their beauty. Experiencing this quality in myself and in relation to and with others has been very important to me in my life. The beauty of what is hidden, it is something like that.

In the process of writing his story, including his dreams, Danville had encountered his own story-teller, his inner Shahrazad, so to speak. "Shahrazad" had healed him like she had done for her husband and his world. And with her, he had found what the Sufis speak of, as the wisdom of the heart.

8

Resolving Fights Between Conservative and Liberal Religious People: The Holy Grail

To me, the Holy Grail is one of the most important images left in Western culture. It still has mystery. The story of the Grail is a myth which is still alive. More pieces of literature have been written about the Grail than any other subject in Western culture. Did you know that this great image may have originated in Persia?[1]

At the heart of the grail are two great images. The grail is the vessel from which Christ drank at the Last Supper. It is also the vessel which was held beneath his body during the descent from the cross gathering drops of his blood as they fell.

The grail is a container. Christ's self-giving is a symbol of beauty and brings beauty to us. The grail conveys the image of holding this holiness and wholeness. It satisfies the imagination to know that the precious blood didn't just disappear, but was conveyed. And conveyed it is, to this day in the image of the Holy Grail. In it we may also partake of the grail's earlier mysteries as well as the indwelling of Christ's image in us.

One object is desired above all others. For those in the Middle Ages, there was nothing peculiar about the fact that the grail was such an object. It was an object that was living-present to an event that transformed history. It is not necessary to be a Christian in order to have some appreciation of the importance of the story of Christ. One part of the watershed of events of Western culture in the ancient world was the transformations, which took place at the Last Supper, the crucifixion, and the resurrection of Jesus.

In response to Jesus' emphasis on service to others, our Western culture has been infused with this ideal. This resulted, for example, in the establishment of early hospitals, care of the poor, etc. Likewise, people through his ideal, have been influenced to develop more fully in accordance with caring for those around them and sometimes for the whole world. Thus human life when inspired by the Christian ideals, has the possibility of transforming the individual and groups within society. The grail is an image of those profound, transformative events (Last Supper, the crucifixion, and the resurrection) which can carry for us the utmost inspiration.

Out of his infinite glory may he give you the power through his spirit for your hidden self to grow strong, so that Christ may live in your heart...until knowing the love of Christ...you are filled with the utter fullness of God (St. Paul).

> Christ is the Grail,
> Christ is the hidden Self,
> The Grail is the hidden Self.

Many speak of the grail as feminine in nature. Its shape is chalice or bowl-like, depending on the tradition one adopts. Both are vessels of holding. There is a tradition of seeing the grail as uterus. Often in ancient paintings, Christ is depicted as held in Mary's womb.

In the realm of the feminine, the imagination is born anew and life is renewed. Wine offered in the chalice reflects the life force. The wine suggests also the ecstasy of intoxication and mystical trance. Further in one version of the grail story, the sacred vessel and a single communion wafer are the entire substance which sustains the life of the Grail King of the Grail Castle.

Thus, in the feminine depths of psyche, imagination is our key to renewed life, and we are sustained in a miraculous way by one essence of the Western spiritual tradition. The grail holds this for us.

As a further note, I quote from C. G. Jung: "The survival or unconscious revivification of the vessel symbol is indicative of a strengthening of the feminine principle in the masculine psychology of that time. Its symbolization in an enigmatic image must be interpreted as a spiritualization of the eroticism aroused by the worship of a woman."[2]

Along this same line, Jung writes: "The medieval background of FAUST has a quite special significance because there was a medieval element that presided over the birth of modern individualism. It began, it seems to me, with the worship of woman, which strengthened the man's soul very considerably, as a psychological factor, since the worship of woman meant worship of the soul."[3]

What could be more ubiquitous and elusive than the feminine in Western culture? Hence, we have the grail's mystery and its staying power as a religious and spiritual symbol and reality.

If I stand up and speak for the grail, I talk of a different reality than the one embraced at the end of the twentieth century. When something is largely missing from dominant cultural values, it is often hard to describe. Yet the grail may, with its bare qualities, throw light upon some of the qualities, vital and sublime, which are missing from our dominant culture. The grail has a decidedly religious significance. It held the wine of the communion and the precious blood substance of the founder of a world religion. As such it is tinged with the mystery of a life representing a profound transformation and the presence of a deity in a human life, potentially in the lives of any one of us today, no matter what our faith or culture. Religious qualities are largely missing from the dominant cultural values of today.

Secondly, the grail represents the prize of an age, at least in the early centuries of the last millennium. In the literature of spiritual poetry, the grail was the most sought after object described in the first, extant written poem describing its pursuit by the famous Knights of the Round Table. Contemporaneous was the building of the great cathedrals of France, including Chartres, dedicated to the Virgin. The goal of this age, in contrast to our own, was a spiritual one.

A third aspect of the grail's value lies in a feature, which is common to all humanity. Some objects and some peoples' activities, in using those objects, actually serve others and moreover can be an expression of love. Giving a cup of water or drink to a guest can serve that function of welcoming, giving and providing for some vital need of another. In my experience such warmth expressed to the guest is a very important part of Middle Eastern culture. Whatever is given or provided to another, when it is infused with service and love makes it have a sacramental quality, celebrating within a common human task, a vital mystery.

Thus the properties of cups and bowls in holding drink and food share by shape, the quality of receptivity, one of the attributes of the feminine. They receive and hold something of value, which shouldn't be just spilled, let go, or lost. Moreover, then serving to bear this to a human being for a vital purpose, completes the meaning of receptacle or vessel. The ultimate vessel, we all know, is the uterus. Perhaps this is another of the associations of the grail with the feminine.

The "Holy" Grail has a pre-eminence among all vessels which serve by holding food or drink. This is because the food of the communion is "the spiritual food of the most high God."

The grail completes, then, something vital in our own age. It compensates the values of our dominant culture. It does this through providing a genuine religious symbol; this includes many meanings, but to mention but two, that of spiritual transformation and the presence of a deity-like quality in the human being. Secondly, the grail reminds us that spiritual qualities were prized above all others in another era, the one which prized the grail above all other objects. This we saw was associated with the feminine as it expressed itself in relatedness, poetry, the arts, and the building of cathedrals dedicated to the sacred feminine, which is also Mother Earth. Thirdly, the objects and activities of giving drink and food are again connected to all humanity, and emphasize the values of service and love. Again the very shape of cup and vessel emphasize once more the feminine, a needed value in our time.

May it not be so that in this symbol of the Holy Grail, mainstream and esoteric Christianity meet?

I close this chapter with two dreams offered to me and to you, the reader, by a young woman.

Dream of Christ Offering the Chalice

I am asleep in the room in which I am actually staying in.
A fishing lodge in the Queen Charlotte Islands. Christ walks into
the room carrying a beautiful, wide silver chalice. He awakens
me and offers it to my lips. I drink the liquid realizing as I do that it is
 his blood
and body in it.

Christ Consciousness

I'm on the cross with Christ. The cross is in the
sky close to the clouds. Christ's head is resting on his chest
in total surrender to his final predicament. I am lying on top
of him—facing him. I look up and see the halo above his head.
The halo continues into the sky, producing an opening through the
clouds. My thought in the dream is that in Christ's ability to
surrender he was able to connect with God.

> I then looked down and saw the people in agony who were
> witnessing his crucifixion. I started to sense in myself
> absolute power as I hung on the cross with Christ, of the joy of
> the spirit of God and also the agony on suffering in the human
> form—and the courage/strength of fiber of the psyche to hold both
> to be
> true. Also a sense of my heart opening.

Isn't it ironic that one of our most treasured symbols in Western culture could have originated in part in Persia? However, there is another very important reason for including the Grail here. Our discussion points to the fact that fundamentalists and non-fundamentalists need to meet. The divisions which have come to be emphasized between Muslims and the West are also divisions between fundamentalists and non-fundamentalists. Those divisions are also present within each group, within Western peoples and within Muslim peoples.

More attention is needed to working with difference *within* Western culture. The Grail, as a place where fundamentalists and liberals may meet, may offer an example for the other conflicts between Western and Muslim cultural groups. As we study more carefully our human values we may find we have more in common with others perceived as different, than we first imagined. The Holy Grail, I believe, is one of the most alive images of Western culture. Isn't it illuminating to think that this image may have first appeared in Persia? The collective unconscious throws up similar images all over the world. You and I participate in that collective unconscious. It can unite us with our sisters and brothers around the world and in every culture.

Notes:

1. I am indebted to Emma Jung and Marie-Louise von Franz for their work *The Grail Legend*, Boston, Sigo Press, 1986. Their understanding of certain key concepts about the grail itself, particularly its feminine aspect, have contributed to my article.

2. C. G. Jung, *Psychological Types*, Coll. Wks., Vol. 6, A revision by R. F. C. Hull of the trans. by H. G. Baynes, Princeton, Princeton University Press, 1976, p. 237.

3. Ibid., p.221.

CONCLUSION

I write at the end of a long journey. In my young adult working life, my preoccupying concern was aiding, in some way, the effort to avoid nuclear war. I worked and lived in New York City during the Cuban missile crisis and throughout the Sixties. My boss and I ran a program that promised to reduce tensions and create better understanding among U. S. citizens and peoples of five European countries bordering the Iron Curtain (Chapter 3). I kid you not that each day was lived with a sense of the importance and urgency of our actions and tasks.

In those days, too, I was trying to learn about the feminine. Jung called this inner manifestation of the feminine in men's lives, the anima, or soul. It is responsible for men's attraction to the opposite sex. Always, in those days for me, there was a connection between these two aspects: creating better cross-cultural understanding and feeling the pull of the anima. When I was most inspired about a breakthrough in cross-cultural understanding, then I would feel attraction for the feminine. This took form in my inner life rather than in outer behavior.

Now some decades from that time, I have reflected again on these themes. I have tried to show in our discussions in this book that the male/female union is an image; that image bespeaks of the union of opposites. It is only a step from that symbolic concept to a deeper notion...that what we call opposites such as spirit and matter for example, are in fact one. This is at the level of reality where, for example, the human observer affects movements of electrons. From this level synchronicities manifest themselves in a way that ties in events of space and time with psychic reality. This was our topic in Chapter 1, on the *Unus Mundus.*

Likewise, it is only a step from that scientific/psychological point to a corollary in human relationships: it is possible, as Bill Kennedy said, that there could be two rights. People from different cultures holding differing views, could each be right. Their views on specific subjects, even issues, could each be right. Living together in one world takes the effort on the part of each of us, to try to inform ourselves on how the views of people of other cultures may be based on their cultural values and symbols which may differ from our own.

One way I felt I might enlarge the understanding of Western people for people of Muslim cultures, was to bring forward some of the literature of the Arab Middle East. I chose the *Tales from the Thousand and One Nights.* Our journey in this book, led us through some of these stories. Such fairy tales and legends emanate as images from the deep, archetypal levels of the psyche that we have just been describing.

In the tale of the merchant, we discovered that in dreams, a way could be revealed to reverse negative fortunes. In Sindbad, we met a man who knew the proper time to resign himself to what was happening to him and to yield up his situation to a higher power. In Shahrazad we learned of the supreme insight of the feminine way, with its power to transform warring tendencies in males.

On one level, treating these stories from a modern, psychological point of view, was a nod in the direction of Muslim culture. On another level, these stories may reveal some truth for our lives.

In the legend from European culture, the Grail, we encountered a similar message to the Muslim tales. In the Grail something beyond reason was revealed that had the power to inspire the highest in human beings such as the Knights of the Round Table, and ourselves. The Grail's essence is so much around us that we may miss it. It is the power of the feminine. That power balances the male traits so dominant in our present world. Careful listening to the other could be considered yin or feminine. Taking into account what we receive by diffuse awareness could be considered like the light of the moon consciousness described by Esther Harding in her *Women's Mysteries*. Reason and power can become very arrogant, as U.S. Senator Fulbright pointed out some decades ago. These attributes need to be balanced respectively by awareness and eros. Each of the males in the world needs to find more of the feminine or yin balance. Males and females alike, need to become whole, in the sense of embodying the best from the masculine and feminine points of view.

We need for these new perspectives to develop along these lines, in order to prevent a power-ordered masculinity from going off the tracks. In the chapter on helping to avert nuclear war, I spoke of dreams. Dreams come from the diffuse awareness realm of the unconscious or psyche. That world is broader than reason and yet includes it. It contains the wisdom of the two-million year old human being that Jung referred to. We need to bring that wisdom to bear on our world problems. It means developing ourselves and expressing ourselves to our leaders. And it means getting psychologically whole human beings in positions of power of all kinds in government. It means having such balanced and whole individuals represented in places where the future is being charted, such as think tanks. It is an immense task to learn and keep learning in our daily lives that even though I may differ from another individual or culture, I can be right, and he or she can be right. Immense, yes, but vital for our future.

The title involves a play on words. I have tried to establish in this book, that in values, the Muslims *are* like us. However, a second meaning is also possible. Maybe if we took an interest in their culture and tried to meet them, they would like us i.e., feel friendly disposed toward us. So much can be achieved by cross-cultural encounter, the meeting of the other. It is incumbent on us to find ways to do so. It can bring healing in the world.

APPENDIX

These poems of mine, I submit as being of a similar spirit to moderate Muslims, as I read their works. The very short prose piece I believe also reflects a similar religious tolerance to be found in someone like Ibn Arabi.

The God-image is not Dead

God is not dead.
Exit twenty centuries
and twenty-five in the East
Even more in Palestine
the tiers of Indians and Chinese,
Such an energy doesn't
roll over and die
e'en if mind would have it so,
Foundations of minds and beings—
The god-image is not dead.

How do I know
I'm not counting on Aquinas
or Plotinus, Plato or Zeno,
The bridge to Newton's lab
is not so widely traveled,
Franklin had his fling
and while Jefferson's logic danced
I'm speaking beyond these,
in the direction of Waldon Pond
and Spring's Great Thaw.

It's time for the great thaw
to come home to us

whether in tones of "emptiness",
Buddha compassion or bliss,
sacred sense of history,
the still small voice,
Shiva dancing the world,
Mahabharata's echoes,
depth analysis
Zen, or meditation.

Or the still small voice
poised by the Big Bang
I know that to which
I belong is not dead
even as I live that
which gives form to formless ideas and
returns again to chaos
that number, that order
among disorder, is mine.

Praise the Jews and the Sufis
Praise animism
and shamanism, Christians,
tribesman, wonderful women,
mystics, Tibetan masters,
late and near wise
persons tuned to the spirit
of the universe, from everywhere,
they can't all be wrong;
more, the frequency alludes the receiver.

Some would rather anything
than anthropomorphism,
and anything we've got,
Hollywood and "image,"
culture's field is vacant

for a supreme idea;
then one not so supreme
moves in, takes over
the lonely house, the hovel,
bereft of any meaning.

There is someplace to look,
to the tenderness of a saint,
to the compassion of Ocean of Wisdom
to the song in the free mind
to the limits of reason,
assonance and synchronicity
subtleties of chaos theory,
one world underlying
matter and spirit,
inner world of Spirit.

If we humans are really
of the stuff of the whole
and awareness has come our way
then we could become
the universe's awareness,
look back on God,
be part of God,
as Meister Eckhart said;
God is not dead, No division, Om.

They said God was dead
with Darwin's evolution,
if only the fittest survive
then no truck with morals;
yet newer science has prove
animal species depend
on each other, upon balance,
relativity's more modern

seance, yet not so
powerful yet as hate.

That is our fate
to stop the bomb in anyone's
hands, the machine gun,
the psychopath's cry
of fire in the crowed theatre,
no matter the slogan;
without the god-image
how are you going to stop
these madmen
some claiming deity's will,

When no one's home at the top,
and the citadel vacant
which used to be reserved
for deity, then
the countryside is in turmoil,
technology doesn't change that,
When will we turn again
to find the god-image within,
Deity's more than
the secular state.

You would have to have
a completely different attitude,
Pindar's human virtues
crying out,
but for that you need
one inviolate,
incorruptible essence
born of the knowledge of good and evil

transcendent over personality
and born beyond time.

An essence beyond religion
and containing its essence,
a flow beyond words
and uttered,
a seeming passion
and letting go,
and experience beyond faith
and faith in experience
and rootedness in life
and knowing the Beyond.

Where is the great thaw?
It is in the human heart
walking by nature's stream
shafts of greenest grass
emerging from warming ground,
the darkest death over
when no sound had been,
presence "walks" beside.
I talk to presence, "prayer"
in another land—before
biology, criticism,
self-consciousness erudition—
at home where the soul
hears its own voice
shake in delight with the new,
a winking star of the universe.[1]

Restoration of the God-image

When I was young, I had the sense of being loved. It seemed the underlying sense of reality itself loved and upheld me. People of various views might call this the image of God in the human being. Some could criticize that this is a naïve and romantic view of life characteristic of an infantile phase. This critic could go on and add that neurosis grows from holding on to such infantile views. The truth, however, is just the reverse. I have not been able to hold onto that sense. Only now as I enter deeply into the second half of life, am I able to remember that I once had such a sense and to return to it in a new, adult way.

It seems that the completion of my life may consist in the regaining of that quality, so that I know that I and others are founded in this love. We do our best work in life when we proceed from that knowledge.

Why am I coming back to this now as I start the process of decisively aging? I have some footing now economically. I have worked hard, and now I may relax those trails which urged me to great effort for the sake of survival. My children have grown up and left home. My skills in my profession have reached an adequate level. I have time for a few days to relax and meditate. Almost immediately after quieting the mind, I pick up a mind-set which places trust in life. Life, my life, seems to have its foundation in a quality implanted in human beings; it is to know that we belong to a greater love and this is the energy pack with which we can begin our conscious lives.

I recall experiencing that my knowing was part of a greater knowing. It was as if I came into it, and was surprised with the realization that it had always been there without my knowing it or acknowledging it. It seemed a quality that made up the whole universe. I had opened a door into a yet bigger reality in which the stuff of love supported me. Further, it gave me a glimpse of itself as being what life was about.

I could go there repeatedly, when as a college student I began to take walks in nature by a stream. This was towards the end of my first year when my faith had suffered a terrible blow at the hands of modern knowledge, from which up till that time in my life I had been protected in my isolated community by the mountains of Appalachia.

Some people might say that this smacks of secular religion, even fundamentalist Christianity. But it is not bound by creed, nor set in any ecclesiastical framework. Nor is it peculiar to any one religion. Similar experiences have been attested to by people from cultures and religions all over the world.

We are of the same stuff as the total impulse which went into our creation. We have in ourselves all the creativity which over millions of years resulted in human beings. If I were to use one word to describe how it feels for me to be connected with all that creativity and potential for human life, it would be love. That is what the experience feels like to me. But I would like to encourage others to put whatever word they like upon it.

There are implications from this for cross-cultural communication. What would it mean to be really connected to others? It would mean to get to know about their past and discover what it is they see in you, and to help bring awareness to this, helping them see that this is a reflection of their deeper self.

As the poet Rumi often expressed, the love of the soul for God is like love for the beloved. That love in its intensity when allowed to be experienced as a fantasy can be an opening for the greatest love to be experienced perhaps with one's true meaning for being in this existence.

All Life a Unity

All life a unity,
said before, I'll say again,
and when by the moaning bar I put forth
and the twee weed lies reed between my teeth
and axemen lie in wait
then shall the fortress cease,
the waters part.

And I walked on dry ground.
and the tweedlebird was heard to sing,
loud and ringing,
by the stream…

The Old Stream
The stream of thought had wounded me,
the courage to be, and the more
I'd thought on it and colloquy
of seminars and far
reaches of reason and
marring of mental sparring—
the agile forgot in bull leaping afar
in Greece;
surcease had come in sleep.

I'd woke in afternoon
to find the door to death ajar
and the whiff of the eternal
caught in my nostrils,
a jingle going like this:
    why death at the end
    what was life then?
    'never before, never again...'

By the Stream
By the stream singing
sweet songs of my youth,
black spirituals bending
the nerves of heaven,
outburstings, cryings
solemn pleas
uttered in birthing, and birthings be.

In the meadows
I take my leave.
I walk among the daffodils,
am friend to the breeze.
Then I find the road,
small white stones broken.
The Roadmender was here,
entertaining children.
I stand by rushing waters
and hear the roar of forever.
These are my friends.
I shall roll them out on my mat
where the last ocean roll beckons
and I am heard no more.

I am. I've always been.
Whither I was before I do not know.
I have been in the election of the dead.
The sparks of my life were
    struggling centuries ago in
    Damascus, and in small prayer
    meetings in England, and later in
    the mountains of West Virginia,
I encompass all my past, dim
    though my awareness be.
My sparks—my best convictions of
what it is to be me—
pray, tell will live on. Those
who experience them be convinced,
even as I have been, by others.

I've walked a never-never lane,
supped at a stream of might advent,
slept where paupers craved the rocks to
    cover them from inward wrath.
I've known the stream of consciousness,
wound the way of disbelief,
known every little crook of ruses,
    bent on ensnaring sparks of life.

I thought of his death.
I saw a thrush.
Life has ceased.
The skies opened:
bright light and tender shade,
mossy rock and water trilled
The Scottish mountain glade.
His Eleusinian field.
The sun gleams

through breaking clouds.
The bells ring
the nine o'clock of
eternity.

Dreams

Body image dreams are
of substance more powerful than celluloid,
more contrived that novels,
wedding times and remote places,
the wise owl of fortune, the seer,
the soul-image who is priceless.

I have knelt by dreams
and kissed dreams,
marched in the streets,
turning over the scenes
as a religious person handles a rosary
or enunciates a mantra.

Dreams have been my path,
Like the glittering night beads
some child has re-found in the forest
and which lead the way back home;
beads, these turns of the mind
glimmering concrescences of all one is.

And lapping the
shore of eternity, like waves
in a moonlit night no one hears
or almost known, are dreams
or so they seem.

Then we wake up and handle them
like children born to us,
handle with affection and care,
not knowing fully whence they came,
knowing only they will grow up
and be our lives.

Taj Mahal II

Thine alabaster turrets glisten,
turning light into liquid,
running veins of purest stone
earth ever yielded of heart.

Never have I known words sharpened
so delicately to follow thy contours,
cresting layers of round loveliness,
following the form of the feminine.

Nor do the muted sounds raised
remain to speak in kind, immortal—
thy ribs have been, and rib cage,
which produced a sound all for all time.

That sound lingers here. In wonder
move it with your turbid finger.

You'll hear the air slice, a
vowel 'ove', vow love.

Immortal this man's devotion
to what he found through noble woman,
through self, through unlocking gates
and walking in the garden of powdered bliss.

You can meet him here still,
unlike the rest of us who left
that divine moment when
heart and body and form joined.
He asks no fare, our immortal.
Only raise your arms in awe
and know when you touch the fair
he, our laborer of bliss, is there.

The Dream That Won't End

I sailed mid ports of life's last recalls;
I sailed with friends our greatest oceans' ends.
The hour of setting sun which none forestalls,
this hour the most cherished for love of friends:
we met again! In life as well our boon
to meet in hallowed room of peasants' inn
with spoons aside for closeness, unspaced like noon,
the holy gathering of kin exceeding kin.

Beyond Jung would trace the plan entire.
The snake consumed its end: Tibet arose;
I saw the summits lift, unveil their fire;
he glowed in lotus pose amidst the snows.
    The dream had chosen these souls in life relief
    to paint a continuum beyond belief.[2]

Notes:

1. David Roomy, *Inner Journey to Sacred Places*, Raleigh, N.C., 197, p.p. 130-134.

2. David Roomy, *Inner Work in the Wounded and Creative, London*, Arkana/Penguin, 1990, pp. 104-111.

978-0-595-35606-5
0-595-35606-0

CPSIA information can be obtained at www.ICGtesting.com
Printed in the USA
BVOW05s1854280415

398084BV00001B/55/P